# YOUNG, EDUCATED
# AND BROKE

# YOUNG, EDUCATED AND BROKE

HOW A QUESTIONING MINDSET
CAN COMBAT THE FINANCIAL
ILLITERACY EPIDEMIC

MICHAEL J. GRUS

NEW DEGREE PRESS

YOUNG, EDUCATED AND BROKE
*How a Questioning Mindset Can Combat the Financial Illiteracy Epidemic*

ISBN      978-1-63730-807-3   *Paperback*
              978-1-63730-866-0   *Kindle Ebook*
              978-1-63730-981-0   *Ebook*

*"Choose Your Habits Carefully,*
*They Decide Your Future"*

-ANONYMOUS

Disclaimer: I am not a financial advisor, and this is not financial advice.

# Table of Contents

---

*Thank you Dad; you made me who I am today.*

# Introduction:
# The Path Forward

---

"Whether you think you can or you think you can't, you're right."

These words from Henry Ford, entrepreneur and revolutionary of his time, outline a simple yet overwhelmingly clear statement of truth (Boomer). No matter the topic or sector of life, the mindset we exemplify is the determining factor in our success or failure. The mindset you embody determines your path forward. It dictates the speed at which you move, and it accentuates the experiences you have along the way. By believing you can achieve a positive life goal, your body, routine, and actions will follow suit in achieving that goal. Equally, when you believe you are unable to achieve a goal, the body and mind will follow the leader and destruct any shred of ambition or confidence.

The state of believing "I can't…" is overwhelmingly apparent in the personal finance space for young professionals and recent graduates. A long list of "I can't do this because" comes to mind for many young professionals because they never had the proper education or guidance on personal finance. To some varying degrees, knowledge is received in passing or offered in a rare seminar at their college or university, but personal finance education is not a priority in the shaping of young professionals. This ultimately leads to a young, educated, and broke professional who is stifled by doubt and fiscal exhaustion when figuring out how to pay bills at the end of the month and save for retirement; toss in the added pressure of incurring student loan debt to pay for a degree and the trifecta is complete.

The very same institutions which are marketed as springboards to a successful career do little to nothing in the way of developing the fiscal brain of young professionals. Ultimately, the price to pay for the graduate comes in the form of tuition, which has tripled in the last twenty years to a current-day average of $35,720 per year (Hanson, 2021). Once a student graduates, they have most likely taken on a lifetime of debt from a school that has not prepared them to handle their money, the same money which is meant to repay the debt that they took out in the first place. It is no wonder, with such little help, that the nature of the "I can't" mindset is so debilitating in the minds of young professionals and recent graduates.

My discovery of lacking financial knowledge, of young professionals and the overall populous, was unveiled to me a number of years ago.

During my time in college, I was the young and dumb kid chasing a dream of financial freedom and a job. Take notice that I did not say a dream job. I was, and still am, of the mindset that I will not be forced to work until I'm seventy years old in order to afford to retire. How do you accomplish that? Well, you get into finance. The murmurs always said there is a ton of money to be made working in finance. So, I was a Finance major with a focus in Investment Management, with the hope of one day becoming a clean-cut, suit-wearing financial advisor.

Fast forward to the summer going into my senior year of college; I found myself in the exact position I wanted. I was interning at a large financial advisory firm, in a tall downtown building, with a career trajectory putting me on the path to achieve my financial goals; everything was falling into place.

My final project for the internship was to build and present a mock financial portfolio to my manager and the branch manager who were supposed to be my "clients." I worked all summer long building this portfolio through research and analysis.

I put on my best suit and tie (I even bought new socks to match my tie), and I delivered my final presentation. I believed this presentation was the gateway to my first job out of school. I was nervous and excited when the presentation came to a close.

What I did not know at the time was that one single phrase would eat away in the back of my mind for the next four years, putting me on the path to writing this book.

I finished my presentation, feeling both confident in my performance and relieved it was over, when my manager looked across the room at me and said, "You now know more about money and investing than 75 percent of the population." At the time, I was just waiting to hear that I was hired, but the gravity of that statement was overwhelmingly concerning.

Think about that. After some course work and spending a single summer reading, studying, and digging into the depths of the financial world, I had more knowledge about this ambiguous world of finance than 75 percent of people out there. This was not just his opinion; according to Possible Finance, as of 2021: "Worldwide, only one-third of adults understand basic financial concepts." Not only is financial illiteracy a problem worldwide, but "four in seven Americans are financially illiterate," and of those illiterate Americans "only 24 percent of millennials understand basic financial topics" (Fu, 2021).

So when people ask questions like:

- What is a stock? What is an ETF?
- What percentage of my paycheck should I put toward my 401(k)?
- How much money should I have saved by age twenty-five?
- What do I need to do to build my credit score?

the overall lack of financial knowledge becomes very clear. These questions begin to ring louder and louder in the heads of young professionals as the clock ticks on and college graduation is long gone.

In the vast landscape of newly graduated youth and people in general, I believe each person is positioned in three different categories regarding financial knowledge and intellect:

1. Quick Learner
2. Quitter
3. Questioner

First is the Quick Learner. These are the people who either have been bestowed the invaluable gift of financial lessons in their youth or have realized the immense power of time and money, and from there they never look back. This person is pointed in their approach, and something clicks with them where they capitalize on the power of financial literacy.

On the opposite side of the spectrum is the Quitter who has written off the world of personal finance and wealth building. Fear and lack of knowledge cripple the Quitter for the long-term as they do not prioritize knowledge building or amassing personal wealth. For one reason or another, the Quitter turns their palms up on the topic and finds themselves living paycheck to paycheck.

Finally, we have the almighty Questioner. The Questioner is curious by nature and has picked up snippets of financial advice, which sparks their curiosity. Knowing there is much more at play, the Questioner lists their personal *Shoulds*: they should be saving more, they should be investing, they should be...and the list goes on. Their knowledge is lacking, but their redeeming quality is acknowledging they can and should be doing more for themselves.

The knowledge deficit is of no concern for the Questioner as they have the highest yielding asset in their portfolio ready to be utilized: their questioning mindset. The Questioner seeks to understand the subject that seems just out of reach, but with each question these people grow smarter and smarter. Questions lead to knowledge, knowledge leads to action, and with action there is progress.

The goal of this book is to solidify your habits as a Questioner and provide tools and frameworks to guide you on your financial literacy path. But, my dear Questioner, that is exactly why you have come, to read and learn.

Your future—your ability to do what you want, when you want, where you want—is directly impacted by the choices you make today. You cannot change the past, you cannot get back any money you have spent, and you definitely cannot get back that five-dollar coffee you "needed," so from this point on your focus is on the future. Your attitude will dictate your direction, so be sure to remain positive and believe in your abilities and strategy. If you believe you can, you will.

Your mission throughout this book is to challenge your current self to provide for your future self. So buckle up and get ready to nerd out on finance.

**CHAPTER 1:**

# The Empty Diploma

---

*"I think college is basically for fun and to prove that you can do your chores, but they're not for learning."*

-ELON MUSK

According to the National Center for Education Statistics, between 2000 and 2018, total undergraduate enrollment in degree-granting postsecondary institutions increased by 26 percent (from 13.2 million to 16.6 million students). By 2029, total undergraduate enrollment is projected to increase to 17.0 million students.

"Go to school to get a good-paying job." This is the obligatory line that is spewed to many young professionals and young adults in the United States, where college and higher-education degrees have become the determined path after high school. More and more entry-level positions in the working world are requiring a simple piece of paper to denote a standard level of knowledge, which unfortunately comes at a very high price and is irrespective of actual competencies and ability. The predetermined path to college comes not from parents and family, but from social pressures and the prerequisites for "career success."

The college education we are meant to receive is often clouded over the course of four (or in some cases five) years by hangover-inducing activities. The diploma most will receive is nothing more than an expensive ticket to enter the working world and begin paying back debt. This ticket has become necessary, not preferred, and overwhelmingly financially burdensome to financially underdeveloped individuals.

Course loads and major specific work is spread over the life of the degree with a sprinkling of other disciplines portraying the guise of a well-rounded education. But a gaping hole remains in most higher education: the introduction of practical financial knowledge and literacy. While students of all majors are required to complete busy work and memorize useless facts and figures, the vast majority of these same college students lack any depth of financial knowledge, "to manage their earnings once they find a job, how to make investment choices about retirement savings plans, or how to handle the receipt of large sums from an inheritance or gift" (Less, 2018).

The lasting impact of churning out financially underdeveloped young professionals is proving detrimental to the crucial developmental years of financial wealth for these very people. The first years of working are the make-or-break years of financial growth and development, not only for habit forming but also for monetary growth. Yet, young people do not "understand the importance of starting early to save for retirement. Young adults need solid financial knowledge to be able to deal with these and other situations wisely" (Less, 2018).

With educated spending habits, a strong saving mindset, and a will to build credit, those years can prove to be the gateway to future success and help combat being caught in mediocrity.

## SECOND LARGEST DEBT MARKET

The current state of student loans is becoming increasingly frightening with every year that passes. The average student loan debt in the United States is north $33,000, which is only a fraction of the $1.5 trillion in total (Cilluffo, 2021). The gravity of the situation cannot be understated. The value proposition of a college degree is being called into question due to the severe debt burden for the minimal trade-off of an entry-level position which, in some cases, barely covers living expenses and the debt repayment.

You might now be wondering why this expensive college degree does not include required classes on how to handle the financial implications of a student loan post graduation.

It is for this very reason that the validity of a college education is being called into question by many, including Elon Musk. As the outspoken billionaire he is, Elon Musk responded to a comment in an interview about hiring at Tesla, that he believes college to simply be a time for fun and to show that students can complete tasks, but it does not prove they learn anything (Hartmans, 2020). The unfortunate truth about college is that it is nothing more than a means to an end—to place you in a job to fulfill a role.

Granted, the burden to bear does not solely fall on colleges and universities to educate their customers on how to properly manage finances in order to repay their crippling debt. The education system as a whole is also responsible to teach students the gravity of the situation and understand the financial obligation they are taking on to attend a certain school. According to CNBC and a study done by the George Washington University School of Business, 53 percent of student loan holders "would make a change if they could go through the process of taking out loans all over again" (Lusardi, 2019).

Undereducated high schoolers are being poked and prodded into attending esteemed colleges in order to find success in their careers, yet they lack any understanding of the nuts and bolts of a monthly loan payment. Across the board, educational reform is crucial to break the cycle of churning out financially underdeveloped young professionals. The student loan repayment is only a fraction in the grand scheme of financial literacy and abilities. Recent graduates are handed a degree, and then step into a full-time role. They are left out to dry trying to repay their mountain of debt, while also trying to save for retirement, create an emergency fund, and invest and diversify, all while trying to remain sane.

## WITHIN CONTROL

Even though there is severe lack of financial education across the board, that does not mean that this lack of knowledge is to remain a permanent state of being. In every situation we encounter in our lives, there are controllable and noncontrollable aspects. Oftentimes we do not recognize or simply neglect to acknowledge the controllable versus the noncontrollable.

Now, let me be very clear. I am not saying whether or not you should go to college; for some people that path is necessary for their career, and for others it may not be. The important takeaway is that, objectively speaking, there is a deficiency of financial education during and post the college level. For those who choose to attend college or have graduated, it is crucial you understand that simply because financial lessons were not taught during your time at school, does not mean that you must accept that outcome.

The responsibility falls on your shoulders to make the best of your current and future situations. And to understand how to move forward, you need to understand there are three buckets that make up your life experience:

- Environment
- Capability
- Behavior

Every action and event in your life can be categorized into one of these buckets, including your financial knowledge and current checking account balance. Understanding the correlation of these three items provides clarity to the causality of your life and outcomes, outcomes simply being the results of actions that are driven by emotion, while way deep down in the secret place, everything is being steered by your value structure (TCCO).

**ENVIRONMENT**

The collegiate path has become the path normalized by the education system and society as a whole. This current environment outlines the structure and path to career success: first graduate high school, pick a college, and secure a job at a company.

Lovely.

The necessity for higher education has fallen under attack in recent years, being called out on the very fact that it is nothing more than a formality for employers. There are people, especially in the rising generations, pulling back the curtain and exposing the flawed system. These dissenters are repopularizing the idea that college is not for everyone nor is it necessary for professional success.

Public figures, business moguls, and self-starters are publicly challenging the idea and necessity of a college degree, especially in the twenty-first century. Not only are there alternatives to pursuing a college degree, such as trade schools and the military—both of which build necessary skills— but according to Tom Ferry, "all the knowledge you need is already at your fingertips" (Hartmans, 2020). A whole host of other successful individuals who have built business and brands speak to this topic by expressing their viewpoint:

Markus Hetzenegger - founder and CEO of NYBA Media

*Back when I was considering whether to go to college, I asked myself where I wanted to be one day and how I could get there the quickest. If I'd wanted a leadership position in a large company, I would have made a different decision. But my goal was to be my own boss and work hard on my own projects, not someone else's. I don't disagree with studying in principle, but if you know in your heart that you don't want to work for any company but your own, you can make better use of your time. While others spent years studying and commuting back and forth between exams and parties, I built a seven-figure company in the same amount of time. I'm not saying it was easy, but it was the only path I could see for myself—and I would choose it again today.*

Brandon Dawson, Serial Entrepreneur and Cofounder/CEO of Cardone Ventures, founder/CEO of Audigy

*I was an average student with a 2.4 GPA. After high school, I moved to Georgia for a sales job with a lot of traveling. I learned to be self-sufficient, connect with others, and sell to professionals. I gained all the skills to survive and thrive on my own—and the courage to never look back. This confidence served me well when I walked away from a lucrative job to start a business as a 27-year-old with two young children. At 29, I took the company public. I later built and sold another for $151 million. I didn't need a degree to teach me something I'd rather learn by doing anyway. I learned by thinking bigger and challenging myself to make a more significant impact. Intentional action creates results. If you're committed, you'll eventually succeed (Hartmans, 2020).*

With such outstanding examples of successful people who hold the stance that a college degree is not always necessary, it is energizing to see their success. But these amazing examples are not only the status of people who suggest college is not the required path. Small business owners, tradespeople, and entrepreneurs big and small support the same tenet. College is not for everyone, nor is it a requirement to be successful, that's just what we have been told to believe in our modern-day environment.

## CAPABILITY

Despite whatever environment you now know, you have the power to take control through inquisitiveness. By elevating your environment, you begin to understand more of what you do not know. So in the world of personal finance and financial literacy, you may not have the best spending habits or saving mindset, but this too is subject to change. You hold the power to determine your path, but the second element that contributes to your overall financial journey is capability.

A perfect example of developing one's capability to change their environment is Graham Stephan, who grew up knowing that college was not his path in life. When he reached eighteen years old, he set out into the world of real estate. He spent countless hours learning his craft not only from on-the-job training but also by research. He remarks that he used YouTube as his outlet of choice and would spend countless hours scouring the platform for any information to help him grow his business and financial knowledge (Graham Stephan, 2017).

As he continued his long hours on the job and his research marathons, his career began to take off. In the real estate market of Los Angeles, the allure of selling multimillion-dollar homes was just out of reach. After years of working late and devoting every ounce of effort toward building his business, he had positioned himself at the Oppenheim Group, commonly known from the show *Selling Sunset*.

With clients such as Orlando Boom and others of similar caliber, his business was established and flourishing. From there as the savvy person he is, Graham took to real estate investing and overall personal finance. After that, he took the platform he had once been encapsulated in for hours a night and started his own YouTube channel.

Now, his main channel has just north of three million subscribers, and his other channels follow suit. With his four channels combined, he collects approximately $270,000 per month in YouTube ad revenue.

As he continues to develop his content and platform, he has positioned himself in the personal finance space, creating content to educate and inspire. Graham Stephen, now part of the 18.6 million people who qualify as a millionaire, is overwhelmingly active in the personal finance space, along with a number of other content creators (Graham Stephan, 2017).

The success story of Stephan exemplifies that even though the current environment is coercing students to attend college for financial success, there are other ways. Graham took inventory of his skills and knowledge and coupled them with what will prove to be the ultimate success factor throughout this book: a question.

## BEHAVIOR

The behaviors that you exemplify on a daily basis are a direct result of your value structure; here comes those feelings again. You have probably adopted values from your parents, teachers, siblings, or any other person who has an influence on you. The values you carry around daily can consciously and, more often than not, subconsciously drive your actions. And this flow goes both ways because "your beliefs and values directly influence your attitudes and behaviors. By digging deep into your character and understanding these concepts, you can determine why you act a certain way. And the best part is, you can go the other way as well. If you don't like how you act in a specific context, you can identify the root beliefs and values and shift them to allow for different actions" (Ionescu, 2021).

There will always be a trade-off in the activities and actions that you part take in; if there wasn't we would all be rich and be able to do whatever. But, as Mark Manson, author of *The Subtle Art of Not Giving a F*ck* explains, you have a limited number of f*cks to give. You cannot give all your attention to everything in your life, just as you cannot give all your money and resources to everything in your life.

Your value structure drives the way in which you allocate your personal financial f*cks. This is a personal shift you must make for yourself. In the present, that new outfit might feel great, but does it feel better than being able to retire three months earlier?

Once you set your course and outline your financial value hierarchy, it will soon impact your capability. You will begin asking more questions of your friends and researching about your 401(k) and investing. After that, you will soon see your environment change; you might not be going out as much, you might enroll in financial workshops, and before you know it, your new values have kick-started the causal chain to financial freedom.

## WHAT NOW?

No matter your opinion of college degrees and the educational system as a whole, there is damning evidence and patterns surfacing about the constant flow of uneducated young professionals. If you fall into this category of young, educated, and broke, you cannot change what you learned in school, you can only control the future.

When you decide to take control of your future and make up for the lost time and knowledge, you can start with addressing your environment, capability, and behavior. These three categories of your life will play an enormous role in your wealth-building strategy. Your journey should begin by questioning everything in order to craft your own money mindset.

Start from within, question everything, and soon your hunger for financial literacy will consume you.

**CHAPTER 2:**

# Why This? Why Now?

———

*"Eighteen to twenty-five: You're either building your foundation or destroying it. Very little in between."*

-JORDAN BELFORT

Time can either work for you or against you; you choose.

No matter if you are speaking about building a career, relationship, or personal wealth, the one unruly constant, the only unchanging and irreplaceable factor is time. Time is invaluable, and it is the chief of all resources. Time does not discriminate, and time surely does not care. It is ruthless yet powerful beyond compare and is both the problem and the solution in your wealth-building journey.

Money will come and money will go, but time only flows in one direction. Financial literacy and wealth building follow the same flow as time. Any moment that is squandered away is lost forever and cannot support the growth of a portfolio. The journey to learn financial lessons that have been missed out on from the past four years of your education should begin as soon as possible, because every day that passes is not only a day of knowledge lost but a day of money lost.

The importance of time in relation to wealth building cannot be overemphasized, it is the end-all be-all and rewards Questioners, those who utilize it to their advantage, for as long as possible.

### WHY THIS? WHY NOW?

"More than two-thirds of Americans have less than a thousand dollars saved up. Worryingly, the majority of those with less than a thousand in savings have no savings at all. Around 45 percent of adult Americans were unable to save any money in 2019" (Urosevic, 2021).

No matter what your current financial status is, it does not affect the message of this book. There are no qualifications or minimums to meet in order to learn and grow your knowledge. Whether you are carrying school loans and making thirty thousand dollars, or you have zero debt and have a starting salary of seventy-five thousand dollars, you still may lack the necessary wealth-building knowledge and habits to be successful. An enormous salary means nothing if you do not know how to manage it properly and spend 90 percent of it.

The race is on to educate yourself as much and as often as possible to right the ship that was well off course throughout college. Whatever position you find yourself in at this moment, it is exactly where you are meant to be. From this point on you will be made aware of your potential for wealth building. By tapping into your potential and harnessing the power of time, you will be primed to win. Although the fruits of your labor might not bloom overnight, your goal is to build sound financial habits in your early professional years to support and grow into the future.

The past is over, and you can only work toward a better future. You can wait another day to begin building your financial brain, but as Joe Sabah, nationally recognized speaker and consultant, remarks: "You don't have to be good to start… you just have to start to be good."

The time is now, and the task is clear.

## I WISH I WOULD HAVE KNOWN…

One of the many intriguing aspects of human nature, chalk it up to either stubbornness or pride, is that too often we neglect the best learning resource we have at our disposal: other people. As young professionals enter the world of financial literacy, it is not necessary to learn financial lessons by trial and error. Everyone has the best teacher and mentor available to them: other people's knowledge. Lessons learned from others are a terrific way to proactively learn and speed up the learning process for yourself.

Asking questions of people who have struggled their way through the unforgiving sea of finance and personal wealth building is the easiest way to capitalize on their mistakes. As harsh as this may sound, you can profit off others' past mistakes and struggles. By learning what to do and what not to do, you can craft your own personal wealth strategy without the monetary implications. Go ask anyone older than you, no matter if they are double your age or a year older, they will recite a laundry list of money-related items they wish they had done differently but didn't know any better.

Money has become a difficult topic to discuss, especially if someone has struggled and learned the hard way through poor financial decisions. They might not want to share because of the fear of being embarrassed. Colin Walsh, CEO and cofounder of Varo Money, addressed this concept of money shame in a *New York Post* article by explaining: "Talking about money is culturally shameful. Everyone needs it, and it controls so much, but no one wants to talk about it." Money, and money knowledge, control so much of the world around us that we need to talk about it in order to learn, but still it remains hush-hush (Wolfson, 2018).

In your endeavors to discuss and seek out financial lessons from others, the only way this can be achieved is through the art of humble inquiry. This form of fact-finding and questioning comes from Edgar and Peter Schein, who explain it in their book, *Humble Inquiry: The Gentle Art of Asking Instead of Telling*. They explain how the cultural practice of information exchange has morphed from inquisitive conversations to task-driven, closed-ended conversations extracting snippets of information. By utilizing the act of humble inquiry on your money journey, it will yield more useful responses.

The execution of humble inquiry requires nothing more than another person to interact with. The opening of the conversation is simply an exchange of humility; this can be your money story that put you on the path to financial literacy.

This offering opens the door for reciprocation and begins the conversation. People want to be heard, and when you approach this conversation through humble fact-finding, soon the "I wish I hads…" will begin flowing. Coupling this humble inquiry approach with proper question forming will help you extract priceless snippets of information from any and all whom you engage with.

The concept of leveraging other people's knowledge for your benefit is not a difficult task. This is the first stop of many on your journey to craft your own money mindset. With every lesson learned from someone else, it will help you along the way in avoiding the same mistakes those who came before you learned the hard way.

## EVERYONE IS ONCE A NOVICE

Developing a financial knowledge base and crafting your money mindset is no different from any other skills that we as humans learn to master. Engineers and doctors attend school and complete rigorous coursework to learn the necessary skills to build structures and perform surgery because they are not born with those skills. Financial literacy is the same; it is a compilation of knowledge and skills learned over years of studying and trial and error.

Earlier I shared with you that I interned with a financial advisor going into my senior year of college. As most impressionable college students are, I was ready to absorb as much information as I could from my supervisor. At the time, he had a well-built book of business clients on which he continued to grow and be successful. He had a great view of the city from his office, he wore tailored suits and enjoyed the career he had built for himself. He was, and still is, doing well for himself.

However, he, too, was once a novice when it came to financial knowledge, business acumen, and networking. He worked tirelessly for years to develop himself to be the advisor he is today because he was a novice at first.

He shared a story with me about when he first joined his company after school. His company offered stock purchasing options, but no one ever walked him through this process; he knew nothing about it. Fast-forward a year and his company was acquired by a much larger financial institution, skyrocketing the stock price of his company, all of which he missed out on. Even financial experts were once novices.

My journey to build my knowledge base will continue for the rest of my life, as there is always more to study. I began with zero knowledge, but through my experiences, such as my internships, degree, and learning from others, I have positioned myself on the path for success.

But I had to start somewhere, and the summer of my internship, my research sessions for my final project would frequently be interrupted by informal coaching sessions with my manager, whom we will call S. These sessions sometimes would last twenty minutes, and other times they felt as if they would never end.

During these coaching sessions, the ad-lib conversation would always begin with some form of open-ended question:

"Tell me something you learned to today?" or "What do you know?" After I spewed out some half-baked response, S would begin his barrage of role-playing exchanges as if I were an advisor and he the client.

Time and again, my pathetic responses left him unimpressed and certainly left me with a list of items I needed to go study up on. But as the summer progressed and the coaching sessions began revealing a method to his madness, I understood his ultimate plan for me: learn through questioning. S, although he was stern, achieved his goal to develop my ability to question upon the completion of my internship. I elevated from a novice through utilizing questions of not only my managers but everyone else throughout the office. I have come a long way from being a novice, but still have more to learn.

## EMPHASIS AND TONE

There is much more to a question than meets the ears. Questions come in all types, form, and tone and can either burst open a conversation or shut it down simply by the structure of the phrasing. A simple question can take many forms of implied voice when the emphasis is directed to a different word. For example, if you read the question below and put emphasis on each main word of the sentence, it takes on an entirely new meaning.

What is your definition of financial success?

If you emphasize *what*, you are seeking an answer of a clearly outlined end state or embodiment of financial success. If you focus on *your*, you are seeking an answer that is tailored specifically to that person, not other people's answers. If you target the word *financial*, you are seeking an answer that is specific to money or wealth, and finally, if you emphasizes*Success*, you are looking for an answer that will be molded by that person's definition.

That exercise only utilized emphasis. Once you combine tone, body language, and every other social and linguistic variable, there are limitless forms of this question. Questions can be insanely powerful when formed and utilized correctly.

As I sat across the desk from manager, becoming visibly frustrated with the circles we had been going in during an exercise, I threw in the towel. I explained to him that maybe I wasn't cut out for this role because for whatever reason I couldn't comprehend how to ask a question.

In this exchange, he was playing the role of a prospective client, a prospect. The purpose of the exercise was to learn as much information about his financial plans, retirement goals, and current financial situation. As I continued to struggle with asking questions, I realized that closed-ended questions were not the answer.

Again, visibly frustrated as it was my third attempt at the exercise, I asked him, "So when do you plan to retire?"

To which he responded, "Sixty-five." Then he sat still, with a blank stare.

So, I asked another question, "How much do you plan to retire with?"

He replied, "I don't know. Aren't you supposed to tell me that?"

I had run out of questions.

Stress and mental exhaustion played a factor, but this exercise was a huge failure on my part. Abruptly, he said we would wrap it up there, and that I should think about how I could improve and try again next week. So when the next week rolled around, we engaged in the same exercise. This time, he told me the roles would be reversed and I would be playing the part of the prospective client.

As soon as he began the conversation with me, the light bulb went off. He opened with a single question. He asked me in a genuinely interested tone, "So tell me about your plans for retirement?" Right away I saw the glaring difference. He had just asked me to open up about my personal life plans and goals through the tactful use of humble inquiry and genuine interest. I talked for five minutes about my interests and what I saw myself doing in my early retirement. I explained how I was determined not to work until I was sixty-five and explained that if money was not a concern, I would open a fishing charter on the coast. He sat silently engaged with every word I spoke.

By asking the right questions, the transfer of knowledge can be limitless. My manager had been crafting this skill his entire career, through trial and error. I walked out of the exercise that day smiling from ear to ear because I had learned the power of a good question. I felt as if I could uncover anything I wanted, simply by framing my questions correctly.

This story has remained the foundation of my financial, personal, and professional journey.

Everyone begins their financial journey in a different place, and everyone at one point in time knows absolutely nothing. Through the power of properly framed and positioned questions, you can elevate your financial brain overnight.

## FINANCE IS PERSONAL

As you begin your questioning journey, the internet and books will be great places to start. You will find answers to questions like, "How much should I be contributing toward my 401(k)?" or "How much money should I have saved at twenty-five?" but this research will not be tailored to your life. The research you will uncover is all driven by averages and cookie-cutter situations, but you and your money are unique.

Your personal portfolio, goals, and aspirations are unique in every sense of the word. So relying on a single blog post, or some advice from a friend, is rather ill-advised. As an educated adult who can reason and deduce upon gathering facts, you must make your own decisions about money per your own financial situation.

As you become more structured in your approach and you refine your strategy, you will see opportunities to adjust your plan accordingly. Your finances are just as unique and intrinsic to you as your identity and personality.

Tori Dunlap of *Her First $100k* says you also need to develop your financial personality. Dunlap gained massive success by quitting her job in corporate America to go on to build a net worth of over one hundred thousand dollars by age twenty-five. She built an internationally recognized financial literacy brand empowering women to wealth as well.

Your financial personality sets a course toward success through compounding steps of building financial literacy.

Within your financial personality, Dunlap emphasizes finding and achieving financial wholesomeness as opposed to financial success. Just as your finances are personal, they, too, must be respective of your life and overall health and well-being. A financially successful person is not financially wholesome if they are continually burned out and unhappy for the sake of money. This financial wholesomeness is the happy medium of building a robust and structured financial personality while remaining human and enjoying the pleasures of life (Marriage Kids and Money, 2019).

Tori Dunlap is a perfect example of a person who prioritized her financial literacy to build financial wealth in the prime years of her wealth-building life. As we will explore later, time favors the invested, and her portfolio would undoubtedly confirm that statement.

## MONEY IS TABOO

Weight, politics, and money. All are very personal and intimate topics, but what is shocking about these is that according to a poll conducted by Acorns, the investing application, from a group of three thousand Americans ages eighteen to forty-four, 68 percent responded that they were more comfortable discussing their weight than they were discussing their money (Grant, 2020). To even further that point, Kerry Sulkowicz, American psychiatrist, psychoanalyst, and professor at NYU Langone Medical Center, explains "...money has long been the biggest taboo—much more than sex" (Feldman, 2013).

Money is taboo simply for the reason of perception and status. Blame it on the societal behaviors which have been passed down from generations or the fear of judgment by peers in modern day, but money can be a nervous breakdown-inducing topic. The tendency to compare ourselves to others runs rampant with social media because it displays the highlights and hides the details. You will never know the actual financial well-being of someone from judging their social media or in even speaking with them because we are so afraid to talk money.

The stigma that comes with talking about money is outrageous; we have morphed into a world where you should only talk money with a spouse or an advisor. But there are millions of other people in the world who have valuable knowledge to share and lessons learned to pass on. So why would you not utilize all the resources at your disposal? Knowledge is only transferred from one person to the next through social interactions, and when done through humble inquiring and genuine interest, there is no telling what those conversations might reveal.

Acceptance and acknowledgment of your current personal financial situation is key. You must first come to terms with whatever your financial situation is, no matter if it is good, bad, or ugly. Your situation is yours, and it has led you to the exact point that you are at today. Your money doesn't define you. What defines you is how you approach bettering your situation. What defines you is how you strive for better every day and rejecting the pressure to remain forever shamed that you might spend a little bit too much.

Taking ownership of your situation in life is when you can make the biggest impact.

Money is taboo no longer. Money questions are your key to financial freedom. The time has come to question everything.

# CHAPTER 3:

# Prisoners of Pleasure

---

*"Don't tell me where your priorities are. Show me where you spend your money, and I'll tell you what they are."*

-JAMES W. FRICK

As humans of the twenty-first century, we have deteriorated and developed into prisoners of pleasure. The theme of instant gratification heightens as we are able to control our lives from phones and laptops. This state of instant consumer gratification, and subsequent monetary implications of dwindling account balances, has evolved to unimaginable levels. Technology and connectivity encompass every aspect of our lives; we have the ability to program smart devices to set up a reoccurring purchase, have food delivered to our doorstep, and use facial recognition to buy anything right from your hand.

Spending money has become easier with the assistance of technology, but with these advantages we have been distanced and disconnected from money. KPMG published a study in 2019 titled, *The Number One Reason People Shop*

*Online is Because They Can Shop 24/7,* that states "fifty-eight percent of consumers shop online due to online opening hours (or lack thereof). The Internet never closes, making it easy for consumers to buy any product at any time. Shopping, for many people, has never been more convenient." The internet has ushered in a new era of online commerce, whereas prior cash was king, and the physical exchange of paper money was a commonplace transaction. One thing led to another, and soon our paychecks became automated, and before we knew it, our money was nothing more than a number on a screen.

Because we continue to eliminate barriers for commerce, the decision to spend money also gets easier. When paper money was exchanged, there was time to reflect on the necessity of the purchase. You questioned whether or not you truly needed that item or service. In most cases now, our pleasure center is stimulated with a quick to tap of the purchase button before we even give ourselves a moment to think.

We bleed money and our hard-earned wages on items we won't use more than once. We have become mindless consumers pushed toward spending by artificial intelligence. What most fail to realize is that every dollar spent on goods and services not necessary for life is a dollar that could be better spent investing in your future.

## THE MARSHMALLOW EXPERIMENT

Instant gratification and nonexistent impulse control is not a new topic today, it hasn't derived from the growing age of technology. It has been a topic of interest for researchers for decades, including Walter Mischel, a professor at Stanford University. In the 1960s, he wanted to examine the deeper ties of instant gratification and lifetime impact, thus the Marshmallow Experiment was born.

The now-infamous Marshmallow Experiment examined and tested the impulses of hundreds of four- to five-year-old children. The preliminary phase of the experiment separated the children into two groups. In Group One, children were subjected to a series of unreliable experiences: "For example, the researcher gave the child a small box of crayons and promised to bring a bigger one, but never did. Then, the researcher gave the child a small sticker and promised to bring a better selection of stickers, but never did." In Group Two, the other children had reliable experiences. "They were promised better crayons and got them. They were told about the better stickers and then they received them" (Clear, 2020).

Then came the main event, the Marshmallow Experiment.

The Marshmallow portion of the study began by bringing each child into a room individually, sitting them at a table, and having a single marshmallow placed in front of them on the table. The stipulation to the marshmallow, which was explained to the child, was that if the child did not eat the marshmallow while the facilitator was out of the room, they would receive a second one as reward. If the child ate the marshmallow at any time before the facilitator returned, the child would not receive a second marshmallow. A rather simple concept: do not eat the treat and get double when the facilitator returns, or eat it now and be happy with only one marshmallow.

The facilitator proceeded to exit the room for a total of fifteen minutes, and this was where the previous experience of the children came into play. Some children tried to fight the urge to eat the marshmallow but failed and only got one marshmallow. Others were able to delay their overwhelming need for gratification and were rewarded with the promised, second marshmallow. The children that were in Group One had no reason to believe the facilitator would honor their word for the second marshmallow and ate the treat, while the Group Two children deduced from their previous experience that it would be worth waiting to receive two marshmallows.

The Marshmallow Experiment hit publication in 1972, where some rather interesting findings were documented from the children as they progressed through life. Researchers remained in touch with each child and followed their educational success and life advances. What they learned was that the children who were willing to delay their instant gratification of devouring the marshmallow produced "higher SAT scores, lower levels of substance abuse, lower likelihood of obesity, better responses to stress, better social skills as reported by their parents, and generally better scores in a range of other life measures" (Clear, 2020).

This experiment continued for forty years, following the same children, wherein the same trends recurred; the ones who found the discipline to resist the urge produced better life results compared to the other group of children. This study has found extreme popularity as of late, and this is but one data point dissecting the human psyche, but the original premise remains: for anyone who wishes to succeed at a certain task or activity, they must find the patience and self-discipline to delay the temporary high of instant gratification for the ultimate gratification of long-term gain.

Being a prisoner of pleasure is nothing new, it has simply transformed. Our current-day marshmallows are now internet sales and "buy five, get one free" deals. The Marshmallow Experiment explored and documented the long-term effects of remaining a prisoner of pleasure.

Although our lives should not eliminate all spending on non-essential items and services, it is exponentially impactful to remain diligent to an outlined budget. One that is supported by constant reminders that delaying pleasure now can deliver overwhelming future financial benefits.

## DISPOSABLE INCOME

When payday rolls around, there will always be bills to pay and groceries to buy. But the money that remains has infinite purposes for which it can be used, which is often referred to as disposable. This money that sits in limbo can be leveraged to save for retirement or can be spent on craft beer or concert tickets as it is meant to be used at the owner's discretion.

I refer to this disposable money as your investable income because it reframes the thought around this sum of money. These small shifts will help solidify your adjusted value hierarchy and drive you to examine all the opportunities for this sum of money that had been previously viewed as spending money.

Your opportunities are limitless with your investable income, but it is important you remain steadfast to your personal strategy. Your investable income is a very flexible number; you hold the power to increase this by adjusting your spending. Prioritize your savings and build the foundation of your financial portfolio (which will be the topic of the next chapter).

## VAYNERCHUK SAYS...

Whether you are involved in the personal finance space or not, you have probably heard of Gary Vaynerchuk. He is the definition of love him or hate him, and he produces extremely thought-provoking content. The only reason his content is so triggering, especially regarding reassessing financial values, is because it is all so true.

The current life most of us live is a result, in some fashion, of the life we had growing up, when we were impressionable. Either we used our childhood as support for the future, or we saw what we wanted to change and took action. The personality and entrepreneurial brand of Gary Vaynerchuk was a direct result of his upbringing.

Born in Belarus, Gary grew up in a poor household with nine family members in a single studio apartment. "We were ridiculously poor... My dad got a job as a stock boy in a liquor store. He eventually lived the American dream and saved all his money. But, a funny thing happens when you don't spend any money for four years. You actually accumulate it. So, he used his savings to buy a small liquor store" (Vaynerchuk,

2013). From an early age, Gary saw the potential of hard work and savings.

Today, his outspoken, and often vulgar, presentations and monologues are plastered everywhere imaginable on the internet. The man has a way of inciting a reaction. In one of his many motivational speeches, he stands posed, ready to deliver some life-changing words of wisdom to wide-eyed, eager onlookers. Instead, what he says is obvious and incredibly simple: examine your spending and your expenses. He passionately continues with, "Everybody lives over what they make; no wonder you can't save money. You apartment is too nice. Of course, you can't save money; your car is too fancy... When you DM me and say … 'I can't, I can't [save money]—the first thing I do is go to their account. Don't let me hear you are broke…and the first story I click on, you're drinking a seven dollar…coffee" (Gary Vee TV, 2019).

The number one excuse of not saving and investing is always the obligatory "I don't have enough money." As most people do, they assume the best solution is adding more income to solve the problem. No. You must reduce spending and expenses, which are the drawdowns on your investable income. Instead of adding more work hours or a side hustle, fix the problem at hand: cash outflow.

As Vaynerchuk explains, you can't hope and wish for the ability or money to be able to save; you must reexamine the purchases and outflows you currently have in order to repurpose that money. No matter who is delivering the message and no matter the inflammatory form they might deliver the message, questioning every dollar that leaves your hand is the only path forward.

## KEEP, CUT BACK, ELIMINATE

Now, we have established that your value hierarchy drives your behaviors and capabilities, which ultimately shifts and elevates your environment. Your spending habits are a physical reflection of your value structure and what you hold near and dear to your heart. Misalignment between values and behavior results in stagnation and decline of your financial progress.

As described, Gary Vaynerchuk falls into the "extreme" category, but that is his educational platform and his brand. In his eyes, either you spend money on something useful and necessary, or else it is a waste and could be saved instead. While correct, as beings of habit we are naturally inclined to gravitate toward a habit of practice. For that we need to break down spending to a more granular level.

Rob Bertman, founder of the Family Budget Expert, describes three classifications of activities to help decrease and or eliminate nonvalue-added spending:

- Keep
- Cut Back
- Eliminate

**KEEP**

A keep is a transaction that supports genuine human happiness. Whether it is an upgraded gym membership or a monthly manicure, the keep items are what you know to be worth the money and support your lifestyle in a positive way. The keeps are meant to draw connection to your personal identity without sacrificing your financial future by partaking in the item or transaction.

**CUT BACK**

A cut back is a transaction that might have become a staple of your routine, like eating out or grabbing a coffee every day before work that isn't absolutely necessary. The Gary V. voice would beat you on the head and tell you to go cold turkey and stop today. The cut backs, by nature, are not overwhelmingly beneficial to your life, nor do they support your financial goals. If you were to stop getting your coffee all together, you only position yourself for failure and then overindulge when you next stop for coffee. The cut backs are just that; they are to be incrementally reduced over time.

**ELIMINATE**

These transactions are clearly defined as a waste of money. They add no value or may even negatively impact your life as a whole and should be eliminated immediately. These transactions are not advancing your financial wealth-building journey in any form (Compton Game, 2021).

Bertman realizes that there are transactions that make us who we are, a hobby or indulgence, but they can be limited and rationed. The Keeps are necessary, the Cut Backs can be trimmed down, and the Eliminates have no place in your life. As you go through your next week, every time you swipe your card or buy something, try mentally sorting it into one of these three categories.

## MAKE $50K A YEAR, LIVE ON $3/DAY

The extreme cases of anything are always appealing— extreme weight loss or extreme couponing—no matter the topic, extreme activities incite interest. One example of this is a YouTuber who has fast tracked his way to the forefront of the automotive and car-related vlog scene. James Strad is a car enthusiast based in Utah who has had a meteoric rise to fame.

Buried deep in his playlist is a video in which he details his humble beginnings and how he grew his once two-hundred-subscriber YouTube channel to a 3.19 million subscriber channel with the ability to buy millions of dollars in exotic cars.

James Strad graduated from college with a finance and accounting degree and soon began working at a high-end ski resort in Park City, Utah. He was disgruntled with his pay; he went into his boss's office, put in his two weeks' notice, and fully expected to get countered with a raise. His manager thanked him for his service, and before he knew it, James Strad was living out of his 2002 Audi TT.

He began chasing a dream of being a full-time YouTuber when he started recording exotic cars driving the streets of

California. For fifty-eight days, he lived with less than one thousand dollars in his bank account, a broken fuel pump in an immobilized car, and barely enough money to buy a loaf of bread and peanut butter to eat.

While still uploading his poor-quality YouTube videos and editing his résumé, he landed a job in an accounting firm making fifty thousand dollars annually. But herein lies the catch; after having lived out of his car for almost two months and eating bread and honey, TheStradman, as his YouTube title reads, decided that since he was relatively happy living off less than three dollars a day, nothing should change once he began making a five-figure salary.

And so he did. James Strad continued to live the life of limitations, saving all his money to devote to growing his business. Year after year he continued this lifestyle, even cutting his own hair. The choice to spend money is completely within your control, but it is up to you to prioritize your financial future over temporary highs and break free the bonds of being a prisoner to pleasure (TheStradman, 2016).

## BUY IT TWICE

My financial mindset and habits have developed drastically from the summer my internship ended to when I began working full time. A simple habit that I have picked up along the way, and remains with me to this day, is the concept of buying twice.

The rule of buying twice is a general practice in auditing personal spending and states that when you are preparing to buy an item (big or small) you should not buy that item unless you can financially buy it twice, without credit. What I love most about this principle is that there are a number of fundamental habits that are intertwined into this rule.

First, if you want to buy something using your investable income, but you cannot buy it twice, it serves as a check and balance to truly justify the purchase. Second, this makes you examine alternative uses for that money. If you are able to purchase the item twice, you begin to question if that money could be spent elsewhere to provide greater value. Third, is my own twist on the "buy it twice" mindset. If I am able to purchase an item twice, I consistently challenge myself to use the money that would be used to buy it a second time and either save or invest that sum.

This addition has taught me to audit my spending while allowing me to feel good about my purchases. This is balance for me in my life.

Finance rules and practices are flexible and will adapt with your personal finance lifestyle. What may seem right to one person might not be to another. Remember, finance is personal. As long as you are bettering your financial situation for the future, while living according to your value hierarchy, anyone else's opinion or remarks about your lifestyle should be disregarded.

This chapter is undoubtedly the gateway to the rest of the book and supports the ideas and lessons to come. Spending money has become easy and will seemingly only get easier. But spending is within your control. It is within your control to reduce your weekly expenditures by 15 percent, it is within your control to eliminate eating out, and it is within your control to make fifty thousand dollars a year and spend only three dollars a day. You are your only proponent and the only one who can provide for yourself, live that way unapologetically.

# CHAPTER 4:

# Saving

---

What is your guilty pleasure? Is it fantasy football or that new reality television series? Can you name every player on a professional sports team, or can you detail the lineage of all the characters from *Game of Thrones*? We all have one or multiple facets of our lives in which we devote time, energy, and brain power. This display of habitual execution of certain tasks shows that we have the capability to be detailed and meticulous for any given activity we put our mind to. So why doesn't everyone do the same thing when it comes to learning about money and preparing for the future?

The consumer drive and materialistic culture that has grown over the recent decades has done a terrific job of bringing consumerism to the forefront, while slowly hushing conversations of financial literacy. Why would people want to talk about how to save money and build for retirement when that money could be used for Amazon finds from TikTok? As we covered in the last chapter, the first step on this wealth-building journey is acknowledging spending, calling it out by name, and addressing how to move forward in a healthy and balanced manner.

As the outflow of money is lessened, by simple math, there will be an increase of investable income in your pocket. Savings is the next stop on the progression to financial freedom.

## "NOT BECAUSE THEY ARE EASY"

When first starting out on a financial wellness journey, nothing is easy, and everything seems to be an impassable obstacle. For those with little to no knowledge of how to address spending and saving, it is all uncharted territory. But every time we are faced with a daunting task, proper planning and determination will prevail.

On September 12, 1962, President John F. Kennedy spoke to the nation detailing the events of the lunar mission and the race to the moon. The world forces were battling one another to achieve something no one had ever done before, and Kennedy proclaimed these words: "We choose to go to the Moon in this decade and do the other things, not because they are easy, but because they are hard, because that goal will serve to organize and measure the best of our energies and skills, because that challenge is one that we are willing to accept, one we are unwilling to postpone, and one which we intend to win" (Podium, 2019).

Your financial wellness and wealth-building journey is your mission to the moon. You have gotten to this point in your life because you know you should be doing more, and while you know it will be hard, you have chosen it. Envisioning your financial future might be difficult, but as Martin Luther King Jr. once said, "You don't have to see the whole staircase, just the first step."

These first steps of constructing your value hierarchy, auditing your spending, and paying yourself first, will lead to more and more fulfillment.

## ONLY HALF THE BATTLE

With more money in your investable income bucket, the joy of seeing results will soon overcome you. Unfortunately, that money needs to be find a better home than a checking account. The questions will begin to pile on with this new-found burden of having extra money:

- Where do I save my money?
- How much should I put toward an emergency fund?
- How much should I have saved by age twenty-four?

Every question that comes to mind is a sign that you are on the right path, but these questions must be prefaced by readdressing our common theme: finance is personal. When I first began my career post graduate school, I was navigating the world of full-time money just as everyone else has, or will do, at some point. I scoured the internet and called upon my favorite group of finance YouTubers to give me the answers I sought, but I never found what I was looking for in those videos.

What I did find was clarity; clarity that my 401(k) contribution amount or my savings rate was relative to my life and my comfort level. After experimenting with different contribution amounts, I found my sweet spot. The percentages I contribute and save are my own, according to how I want to live and build for the future, it was not a plug and play scenario from a single article I read online.

## WHERE SHOULD I SAVE MY MONEY?

Under your mattress is not the answer. A savings account is a very ambiguous term, and it makes sense why it can be so overwhelming as to which bank or specific account to choose for savings. The answer to the question, "Where should I save my money at?" again, is a function of your personal needs and current levels of savings.

Liquidity needs are of major concern for almost anyone; having access to cash quickly is one of the main purposes of a savings account, but within that umbrella term, "savings account," there are two paths. Liquidity needs can be achieved in most cases by simply using the savings account that was set up for you when you went off to college. That account will keep your cash on hand to serve as your emergency fund in times of need, but the honest truth about that account is that it is costing you money.

Savings accounts operate by you depositing money into a bank, which then lends that money out to other people, and the bank will pay you interest for doing so. But that interest rate is next to nothing, and the value of that money is slowly decaying from inflation, which we will discuss next chapter. So building a comfortable but not overly stacked emergency fund in this liquid account is a great step in securing your financial fort.

Now if you put on your imagination hat for a minute, picture that you are the CEO of a company. You oversee all the employees, and they report to you. But in this scenario, all your employees are every dollar that you own. Therefore, you would like your employees to be as productive as possible, right? In the example above, the utilization of the very liquid savings account does not have your employees working hard for you, but they are necessary to the operation.

So with all your remaining employees, you would like them to pick up the slack. When liquidity needs for a rainy-day fund are squared away, you can begin building in a high-yield savings account. The internet has opened up a world of possibilities for banking and finance applications; utilize it. A high-yield savings account will be your best friend in the beginning stages of your wealth-building movement, and they can be found almost anywhere.

There will always be pros and cons of different banks and accounts, but make the decision based on your personal finance situation. Having multiple accounts to fulfill multiple needs of liquidity is a great option. The goal is to make your employees work for you and be as productive as they can be, all while gaining more and more employees.

## THE ENVELOPE SYSTEM

Shannah Compton Game is the creator and host of *Millennial Money,* a financial-centered podcast that hosts an array of guests discussing financial literacy and money-minded topics. An episode that made a lasting impression on me featured Jeanette Pavini, author of *The Joy of Saving,* which discusses secrets to finding joy in the act of saving money. Pavini, a single mom and daughter of an Italian immigrant couple, learned from an early age that saving money is possible in any situation.

Pavini details her experiences watching her parents meticulously save and provide a beautiful life for her and many siblings. When she was growing up and her parents were starting their family, it was just after World War II and cash was the primary source of monetary exchange. Pavini's father, Galdo, cemented his financial habits early on in life through the Envelope System.

As mentioned in the previous chapter, technology and online money has disconnected us from our money and ultimately our spending. We do not grimace when we spend three hundred dollars online, but we second-guess ourselves when we physically need to hand over forty dollars. Galdo Pavini capitalized on this physical connection to spending. So every paycheck, the total amount was divided, in cash, into a number of envelopes. These envelopes would include categories such as: Groceries, Rent, Entertainment, etc. Meanwhile, the money they determined was savings was taken out first, before the remaining money was divided into envelopes.

Whenever they needed the money for groceries, they would draw down from the balance in that envelope. Once the money in each envelope was gone, it was gone. Jeanette remembers a number of times when they would live off of macaroni and cheese because the money for groceries was gone for that time frame. Ultimately, this envelope system worked its magic for Galdo and his family, leaving his late wife a large estate to support the family after his passing. Jeanette believes and highly recommends this system of calculated spending and saving to anyone she works with in her financial literacy platform (Compton Game, 2021).

If spending and saving money has become nothing more than a touch of a button, the Envelope System might be the answer for you. The physical exchange of money makes you question your purchases, it makes you value each dollar more and recognize their potential of being your employee and not spent.

## PAY YOURSELF FIRST

If you noticed in the story about Galdo Pavini, when they would use their envelope system, they would withdraw the money they denoted as savings right away. The family would then allocate or budget their remaining resources. This is hugely important in the effort to save money, because if saving is not made the priority, it will never receive the needed attention.

The act of paying yourself first not only helps you monetarily, but it reorganizes your financial brain. This act of saving immediately is highlighting that you are putting yourself and your future at the forefront of all your decisions. This might not seem groundbreaking, but as you condition yourself to doing this with savings, this logic will trickle over into every other category of financial wellness and wealth building.

Second, the act of paying yourself is beneficial because it implements self-set boundaries. Let's say that you received one thousand dollars every two weeks from your job. By paying yourself first, you have decided that you will put away two hundred dollars; this means you now only have eight hundred dollars to live off for the next two weeks. The first months doing this may be bumpy, but you will soon feel out the sweet spot of expenses and spending.

Paying yourself first combats the normal scenario that runs out in perpetuity for most people: you get paid and then pay off all your bills, you buy groceries, you fill up your gas tank, and then you don't have any money left over to save.

Savings should never be "what is left over"; it should be the first account you contribute to each paycheck. Your savings is your future, and if you continue with the mindset that you will save what is left over, your future lifestyle will reflect it. Pay yourself first in the form of savings in the most suitable savings account for you; do not rob yourself by paying for life while neglecting to save for your future.

## 50-30-20 v. 40-30-30

Determining your level of savings rate is highly dependent upon your personal situation. You can research high and low and will inevitably come across a number of suggestions or "rules" for savings. Senator Elizabeth Warren popularized the 50-30-20 rule in her book *All Your Worth: The Ultimate Lifetime Money Plan* summarizing:

- The 50-30-20 budget rule is an intuitive and simple plan to help people reach their financial goals.

- The rule states that you should spend up to 50% of your after-tax income on needs and obligations that you must-have or must-do.
- The remaining half should be split up between 20% savings and debt repayment and 30% to everything else that you might want.
- The rule is a template that is intended to help individuals manage their money and save for emergencies and retirement (Warren, 2006).

This template for savings is a great starting point; it helps bring definition to the ambiguous world of shifting expenses and floating numbers. The next step is to challenge this 50-30-20 rule and strive to reduce your expenses by 10 percent and save the additional money.

Both these frameworks are great rules for savings and a starting point; they provide the initial jumping-off point to kick-start your savings process. I began using both of these, first starting with the 50-30-20 and then moving on to the 40-30-30, and I have since taken my savings rate even further, because it is personal! Instead of saving to percentages set by others, you must craft and execute to your personal value structure and goals.

## THE UNCOMFORTABLE LEVEL

Right, wrong, or indifferent, the life you will live in your later years is a direct reflection of your young professional or foundational years. The amount you save today will directly tie to your future level of comfort and purchasing power. So when deciding on what percentage to save, use your goal of being financially free early and save a percentage of money per paycheck that is almost or is uncomfortable.

Why do I say that? Living close to the bounds of your budget for the foundational early years of your wealth-building journey is the key to amassing capital. If you make fifty thousand dollars a year, you should live as if you make thirty-five thousand and save and invest the difference. Once you have determined your savings rate, stick to it and remind yourself of the final goal, financial independence. The money meant for saving every month is not nonnegotiable or is not to be touched. There may be some expenditures that you can't imagine living without, but discipline your financial brain to live without them for six months and see those savings add up. You will never look back.

Not saving money is not acceptable; you are only robbing yourself if you decide to "save what is leftover" instead of paying yourself first.

# CHAPTER 5:

# You Can't Save Your Way to Wealth

---

"Investing in the stock market is the same as gambling." If you ever hear someone say this, that person is simply uninformed. The number of young adults who own stocks is actively growing. Only 22 percent of US citizens under the age of thirty-five owned stocks back in 1989, whereas over 41 percent did by 2016. Investing in financial instruments, be it stocks, bonds, derivatives, or triple leveraged ETFs, is not equivalent to gambling (Schrager, 2019). For the sake of simplicity within this book, we will be referring to the stock market as the general term to describe platforms by which financial instruments are bought and sold.

If I were to walk up to a roulette table in Las Vegas and put one hundred dollars on red, I would have a fifty-fifty chance of either winning and doubling my money or losing and walking away with nothing. The stock market is not the same; it is built on due diligence, not gambling.

The stock market is not a roulette table. If a new investor decided it was their time to expand their financial knowledge and grow their wealth, and they decided to buy stock, their experience would be much different from the fifty-fifty chance on red.

Let's say our Questioner decides to buy a piece of ownership of a well-established company named Young, Educated, and Broke Inc. (YEB) and that single piece of ownership in the company is called a share, and this particular share cost one hundred dollars.

Upon purchase of that one share, our Questioner would own a fractional part of the company, and that share of stock would hold intrinsic value from the overall value of the company. Through good times and bad times, YEB will see price increases and decreases with the flow of the market and company innovation and performance. There are no guarantees in the stock market, but the likelihood of this established, well-performing company going bankrupt is unlikely. Therefore, the share of stock our Questioner holds has proven a clear difference from a spin of a ball in Las Vegas.

## INVESTING AND HEALTHY LIVING

Living a healthy lifestyle is a very ambiguous phrase that is used to encompass a range of topics. A healthy lifestyle might mean strenuous exercise with detailed dietary restrictions for some, or it might be going for a walk every afternoon, or not having that second piece of cheesecake. Although there are limitless avenues to pursue a healthy lifestyle, there are a number of tenets about it that do not and will not change.

A healthy lifestyle, in whatever form and function it takes requires practice and time to develop the habitual nature that is necessitated by the very idea. A healthy lifestyle cannot be done for three days and forgotten about, that is just a healthy three days. Living a life centered on healthy-minded activities becomes easier and easier the longer you partake in the activities you associate with this lifestyle. It is easier to refrain from the activities you know you should not do after having practiced that for months and years coupled with compounding will power.

With the goal and actions to live a healthy and active life, the decisions that are made to advance that goal will also trickle into other buckets of your life. Your behavior and your environment changes as a result of your altered value structure.

Investing mirrors this idea of living a healthy lifestyle. At first, it may be difficult to branch off from your normal routine and adopt new habits of allocating more money to an investment account, but it will soon become second nature. When you start to reprioritize your life around this investing lifestyle and mindset, other aspects of your life change; you are more mindful of your budget, you will be more cognizant of the amount of money spent, and your life improves.

Just as compounding success bares its fruits for those who chose a healthy lifestyle, the same is true for investing. For the people who find themselves in a doctor's or financial advisor's office, they might get the wake-up call that they need to lose weight or buckle down and reassess their financial situation to have a life worth living. That news is always difficult, because oftentimes it comes later in life, when the most valuable asset, time, has vanished. We are creatures of habit who need routine to break the bad habits that have been cemented over time. That is a tall order to fulfill, so why not start now?

The world of investing is not a "closed door" society; it is open to all and rewards the Questioners—those of you who are reading and saying, "I should be investing." This is your call to action.

## INVESTING IS A UNICYCLE

As we mature in life, the topics we find ourselves discussing change drastically. Before you know it, while at the weekend cookout, you and your friends are discussing investment strategies and talking finance. As you dip your toes into the world of finance, you might not be able to contribute much to these conversations, but as you continue your Questioner lifestyle and dig for new information, you will soon experience the success of the Competence Loop.

The Competence Loop concept explains the compounding effect of achieving small wins and overcoming fear. Kevin Eikenberry, Chief Potential Officer at The Kevin Eikenberry Group, explained this loop on the *Millennial Money Podcast*, relating it to a bicycle and a unicycle. If I were to give you a bike and offered you to ride it, you would have no problem because you are accustomed to riding a bike. Since you have no fear of riding the bike, away you would go into the sunset. But if I were to hand you a unicycle, you would be hesitant to ride and might even reject the idea because it's different.

The unicycle (investing) is similar in fashion to the bicycle (saving), but it is seemingly a new task all together. The only way to get better at riding the unicycle is to go ahead and get on and work toward competence and success. Action is the driving factor in this scenario, and with the internal push toward action you will begin to try more things and succeed (Eikenberry, 2014).

The first time I rode the unicycle of investing, I opened my first investment account. I was equally nervous and excited to be getting out on my own and being a part of this grandiose world of investing. I was going through all the steps to create my account and made my first deposit from my savings. I was set.

Little did I know at the time, or at least neglected to read, my money did not instantly appear in my new investment account; there was a two-day settlement period for deposits. I wasn't aware of this though and was losing my mind. I was in a state of panic and thought I had gotten scammed, losing my three-thousand-dollar deposit.

New things are scary, but we can only learn by doing; I, in fact, did not get scammed, and continued to grow that account, now with a fond memory every time I opened it. Investing competence comes with each small win along the way, compounding not only returns, but also knowledge.

## "BECAUSE YOU CAN'T SAVE YOUR WAY TO WEALTH"

As we have covered, a crucial piece to your personal financial wholesomeness is savings. Your savings are a necessary cornerstone that you will build your financial house upon. But diligently saving in a high-yield savings account does not complete your financial strategy.

If you save four hundred dollars a month for thirty years, you'll have $144,000; how awesome is that?

You have developed your financially responsible muscles and gotten to a place to save early and often in the amount of four hundred dollars; that is terrific, and you should be so proud of yourself. Unfortunately, though, putting all your money toward savings will only prove fractionally fruitful.

There are more factors at play than simply just saving money.

Not only is a savings account going to return marginally, compared to investment instruments, you will in essence be losing money over the long-term because your savings account won't beat inflation. Investing helps to combat these downsides.

Inflation is the declining purchasing power of a dollar over time. This make more sense if you have ever heard someone say, "When I was young, I could go see a movie for nickel," or something along those lines. Our money is worth less year over year, and stories like that help to provide a track record of inflation.

Historically, the inflation rate is around 3 percent with influxes of highs and lows; therefore, you need to position yourself to combat and beat the inflation rate to continue to grow your nest egg. There are options in the high-yield savings account space that can offer interest rates of 0.50 percent, on the high end. For a lot of other savings accounts linked through your checking account, you are earning next to nothing for your money, and definitely not beating inflation.

Inflation is constantly eating away at the money you work so hard for, and your savings account is paying you pennies for having your money tucked away. So what do you do now? Let's say you took the same four hundred dollars and invested it each month for thirty years, assuming a historical return of 8 percent.

If you invest four hundred dollars a month for thirty years, you'll have $1,100,000.

This difference between saving and investing is astronomical and makes the case for investing. Obviously, not everyone will be able to invest this amount each month, but the key is the action and practice. If your personal finance strategy allows for fifty dollars a month, then so be it. But time invested is worth much more than investing four hundred dollars every month in ten years when you can "afford it"; this is the power of the time value of money.

## LEVERAGING TECHNOLOGY FOR GOOD

We have more computing and operational power in the palm of our hands with the latest smartphones than NASA had at their disposal when they put a person on the moon. This technological power is neither inherently good nor bad, but how we use the power is the deciding factor.

As we have seen, technology has done a number of things to our economy. It has minimized the physical aspect of consumerism; we can order alcohol or a car on our phones while sitting on the couch. Even though we are so disconnected from our money, we can actually use that to our advantage by leveraging the same technology in a positive manner for routine wealth building.

Investing has never been easier, with virtually every barrier to entry (no trading fees, the introduction of fractional shares, etc.) having been removed. Financial institutions that have investment (brokerage) accounts have apps for your phone, and you can have your account set up within a few days. By utilizing your power of questioning, you can begin your research and decide the best investment strategy for yourself. The real benefit of the technology comes from the power of automation.

Once you begin your investment journey and have your investment amount decided, you can automatically invest those funds every paycheck. This way, the money is out of sight and out of mind. You never see those funds in your checking account on payday, removing the temptation to carelessly spend those funds.

You can even take the power of automation one step further. For example, Acorns is a trading and financial platform that grew in popularity for rounding up a given purchase of $5.50 to an even $6, then investing the $0.50 in your investment account. You are going to be spending that money anyway, so the extra fifty cents is menial in your in mind, but that

fifty cents will grow and compound with all the other fif-
ty-cent deposits.

Technology is infinite in its power, and it can undoubtedly
transform your wealth accumulation strategy.

## TIME VALUE OF MONEY

It is very ironic that built into the retirement planning process there are exemptions for catch-up contributions. The
very fact that the system acknowledges people have not contributed enough to their retirement, and that acknowledgment is built into the system, highlights the fact that people
don't realize they are on their own. Let me explain.

Every year, in a 401(k) plan through an employer, an employee
is allowed to contribute a maximum of $19,500 without being
additionally taxed. You can, in theory, put more than this
maximum, but you will incur other taxation on those funds
contributed. For employees who are age fifty and over, the
allowable maximum, as of 2021, was increased from an additional six thousand dollars to sixty-five thousand dollars (for
a total of twenty-six thousand dollars for that age group), and
these are ironically named "Catch-up Contributions."

So for people who are nearing retirement and are realizing
they are not as well-off as they might have thought, they
can contribute an additional 33 percent to their retirement
account. On the surface this might appear to be a great benefit available, but it's simply just a Band-Aid to the real problem: financial literacy and the lack thereof.

The Catch-up Contributions are a great way to add additional funds to a person's retirement account as they near retirement, although the time value of money principle explains that these contributions are almost pennies on the dollar compared to if they had invested more twenty years prior. What ends up happening is people who elect to use these catch-up funds of sixty-five hundred dollars will be saving money, today, that is worth less than it was twenty years ago due to our dear old friend inflation (IRS, 2020).

Essentially, by neglecting to save in the developmental years right out of school and deferring until later in life, you will be saving money that is less valuable later in life. Even though you are saving an additional 33 percent, it cannot compete to what it could have been. Once you realize the power of time in this equation, the mere idea of catch-up contributions are almost laughable.

Although this option helps people add more funds to their retirement, usually by this point people have very few choices left since time has been lost. The icing on the cake with the time value of money and examining the compounding over time comes when you look at starting today versus starting in twenty years.

To anyone who believes there will always be time to save in the future or you believe retirement is so far away why should you worry about it now, take a look at these numbers.

Per Acorns, with five dollars invested each day with a 6 percent annual return until age sixty-five, if you start your retirement savings at age:

- Forty-five, you will have $71,210.47
- Thirty-five, you will have $153,042.81
- Twenty-five, you will have $299,592.08 (Acorns, 2021)

The time value of money is powerful. It favors the disciplined and punishes those who delay. With only five dollars a day—or refraining from one impulse fast-food purchase a week—and starting at age twenty-five, you can have over a quarter of a million dollars socked away for retirement. Tomorrow is too late to begin your retirement savings. It's never too early to prepare for your future.

Having seen the time value of money and hearing about the Catch-up Contributions, the quick-witted Questioner might think to themselves, "There is opportunity there." Correct. Those last-ditch-effort contributions are not only reserved for people who neglected or did not prepare for retirement, they are available to everyone. So, when the time comes and you reach the big age of fifty, you, too, can utilize these catch-up contributions.

Now for some, you might question why you should utilize the Catch-up Contributions if you just explained you are saving at decreasing rate. The second factor at play in this equation is the exponential growth curve. Exponential growth is "growth whose rate becomes ever more rapid in proportion to the growing total number or size," simply the proof is in the savings and over time the value will rapidly stair step (Lexico).

If you were a person who needed the catch-up funds, you would not have the nest egg of retirement savings built up already and would be trying to reap the rewards of compounding growth, at a declining rate. But, if you had done your planning and preparation by investing ten dollars a week since age twenty-five, your exponential growth curve will have already been built out. Therefore, utilizing these contributions will only add favorably to the already healthy growth curve and further solidify your retirement savings.

Retirement planning is not limited to any age, and it is not limited to any income level, but it is limited in time. Time will always be the deciding factor. So by prioritizing the future during the present, by exchanging that takeout meal for ten dollars a week toward retirement, your money will go much further then you can imagine. Your value hierarchy will be the driving force behind this simple exchange of product for financial planning, and your future self will be forever grateful to your present self.

## SO WHERE DO I START?

There are endless social media accounts and content producers who have skyrocketed in popularity because they are transferring this world of finance and investing into consumable and enjoyable content. You do not need to crack open a textbook to study the mechanics of options trading because you need to start simple. As you grow your financial vocabulary, your intrigue will get the better of you. Your questioning mindset will send you on the path to discover the things you don't know in the endless world of content.

Now, deciphering this consumable content and utilizing in your own personal investing strategy will take a bit more time and effort. The internet thrives on clickbait and driving hype toward content, whether that content is sound financial advice or not. Oftentimes, you will even see a preface to these videos and blog posts that these people are not financial advisors nor are they providing financial advice so you must take what they say with a grain of salt.

After you have done your research and digging, you will take the leap to begin investing. You have so many options to choose from, providers of brokerage accounts and other financial services. Ask your friends what they use and like or dislike. Research and decide for your personal reasons, not because the talking head said to do so. If all this still seems overwhelming, seek help from a professional advisor. There are limitless and ever-changing options to pursue in the journey of investing, the only constant is the need for action.

## TIME IN VS. TIMING

Whenever you discuss the topic of the stock market and investing, the name Warren Buffet makes its way into the conversation. As an investor, his net worth growth chart is the definition of exponential. He is outspoken and revered as a market indicator in and of himself, and his words and actions send shock waves throughout the financial world.

Just as any influential person does, Warren Buffet has a plethora of quotes pertaining to investing, but there is one in particular that has always resonated with me and guided my financial journey. He sheds light on investor behavior as being a vital piece in the success of wealth accumulation,

"The stock market is a device for transferring money from the impatient to the patient" (Lighthouse, 2017).

Investing is a two-act play. The first act is the setup and the introductory piece, when you establish your routine and your investment amounts according to your budget. The second act is the unfolding of the events over a length of time. The second act of the play is where the patient investors are rewarded. Investing success for young professionals is a function of time in the market coupled with the Competence Loop. Beginning early and often will kick-start the journey of those small financial wins and milestone achievements.

The biggest hesitation toward the stock market and investing is the idea that it is no different from gambling and you have the potential to lose all your money. The latter is indeed a possibility but unlikely. Due to this hesitation and misguided assumption about investing, those same people will be the ones who try to scheme the proven formula for success. Timing of the market is a tricky game to play, with the majority of market gains coming during ten good trading days, and predicting these days is very difficult (Stevens, 2021).

Patience is the key to compounding success. By following this strategy, Warren Buffet grew his net worth from twenty thousand dollars at the age of twenty years old to $1.4 million at thirty-two, all the way to $58.5 billion at eighty-three. Time in the market will beat timing the market (Chang, 2021).

Although investing in the market might not make you as wealthy as Warren Buffet, the underlying principles are solid and will help drive you toward your personal financial freedom.

## "IT DOESN'T TAKE A FORTUNE TO MAKE A FORTUNE"

Small habits breed large victories as you formulate your financial lifestyle, just as they would for a healthy lifestyle. As you begin, or continue your financial journey, everything you do is relative to you. If you cannot invest four hundred dollars a month, that does not mean you don't start investing, it simply means you adjust for your given situation (Hewitt).

As you build your routine of investing, aided by automatic investments and capitalizing on our societal disconnect from money, you are solidifying your future day by day. The money will come, but without sound habits and a defined strategy, your goals will be hard to achieve. As you can see from Buffet's wealth curve, he started somewhere around where you might find yourself today, in your early twenties. Warren Buffet realized and capitalized on time invested and that is why he is able to have such a profound impact; he lived and succeeded by it.

The only thing left to do is to take action. Every step you take today is more valuable than you can imagine. You will increase your earning level and you will solidify your investment habits, but you will never be able to get back time. Time spent floundering about investing is time wasted. Take action today.

## WE NEED FINANCIAL LITERACY

The maturing generations in the United States need to develop sound financial literacy now more than ever. With our unbreakable connection to the "buy now" button and a culture of liabilities over assets, the direction will prove dire for the uneducated. Take for example a tweet from @ InvestingAuthority, one of many content pages in the investing and personal finance space. "Apple AirPod Max is $549. Someone with less tha[n] $1,000 in savings and credit card debt already preordered it. Not knowing that Apple shares are less than $200. They can have Apple make money for them but instead they make money for Apple. This why we need financial literacy" (Investing Authority, 2021).

For younger people or recent graduates, you may or may not have a financial advisor or are using a family advisor. If you are so lucky, continue to ride that wave and meet with them as often as possible because that is what you are paying them for at the end of the day. For others, investing might be uncharted territory and seem difficult to engage in but utilize the wonderful world of the internet to help teach and guide you. YouTube is a great place for tutorials and how-tos of opening accounts and getting invested, so substitute one episode of Netflix and watch a YouTube video on how to get started investing.

Invest in yourself by asking questions and building your knowledge portfolio; invest in your future by building your financial portfolio.

# CHAPTER 6:

# Adult Report Card

―――――

Credit is like dating. When a relationship begins, there is not a lot of substance; there are two people who get along and decide to take the next step. Both parties to the relationship are a bit weary; maybe for one of them it is their first real relationship and they are very nervous about messing things up. For the other person, maybe their last relationship created a lot of trust issues, therefore they are reserved and need to gain trust in the other person slowly and over time.

Months, and soon years, go by of being on time for dinner dates and showing up in times of need. Both people are actively engaged in the relationship, communicating their feelings, and making their best effort to help the relationship grow. Slowly the partner who was hurt before begins trusting again and opens up more and shares more of their heart. The more each party is involved, more open, honest, and dedicated to fulfilling their duties in the relationship, the better it works out over the long-term.

Credit may seem as fickle as relationships sometimes, but when you understand the formula that derives your credit, you are primed to make it work out for you long-term. And while I may have input to give you on credit, I can't say the same about relationships; sorry about that.


## CREDIT DICTATES

Similar to your time in school when your report card, or grade point average, was the almighty reflection of your work, credit serves the same purpose in your adult life. Not only did your grade point average help you gain acceptance to schools of your choice, but it also might have helped with gaining access to academic scholarships for decreased overall college cost.

Regardless of your opinions about the classes you took or the professors you had, the determining factor in everything was your grade point average. It even dictated the designation you received upon graduation, and it never went away. Credit is the equivalent of your adult grade point average. With good credit, you gain access to better financial options, and are offered better deals. With poor credit, the negative implications are burdensome.

Your credit is controlled by only one person, you. This metric that is impacted by your financial discipline is used as an indicator to external institutions as a signifier of your debt repayment ability. A good or bad credit score dictates whether or not you receive optimal borrowing rates, the amount of money you can receive on loan, and a number of other financial facets. Needless to say, it is a big deal. Good or bad, credit is within your control but takes discipline to turn it from a liability to an asset.

There are five categories that contribute to your overall credit score, all of which are within your control:

- Payment History
- Credit Utilization
- Length of Credit History
- Credit Mix
- New Credit/Inquires

These categories play an important role in generating your adult report card to financial institutions. In this situation, a Questioner might ask, "How can I improve my credit?" The answer is simple: control and discipline within each of these categories.

The below percentages are used in calculation of your FICO Score, which is the most popular reporting metric.

1. **Payment History (35 percent)**: Contrary to the stock market and financial instruments, past performance is a relatively good indicator of future results when it comes to credit repayment. On-time payments are crucial to building credit, as it shows lenders how likely you are to repay what they are owed. Remember, credit cards are a tool to better your financial situation, and you should only spend what you are sure to repay in full and on time. One missed payment might not seem to be a huge deal for some, but it speaks volumes on your credit report. Payment history accounts for 35 percent of your FICO score, so take heed of this when you have aspirations of buying a home one day.

2. **Credit Utilization (30 percent):** The term credit utilization refers to a ratio that indicates how much of your available credit you are using while still making on-time payments. "Your credit utilization ratio is calculated by dividing the total revolving credit you are currently using by the total of all your revolving credit limits." (Resources, 2021) This ratio, when under 30 percent, is deemed a good ratio because it shows that you are not using an exorbitant amount of credit proportional to your credit limits.

3. **Length of Credit History (15 percent):** Credit, investment returns, and the perfect chocolate chip cookie, all take time. These things cannot be rushed, and the benefit of the final result is well worth the hard work and the wait. A credit score is a function of the above listed categories, but time is the most valuable resource on the credit-building journey. If your credit is not so great, focus on starting as soon as possible because you cannot rush time. You cannot purchase a better credit history.

   a. Experian, the multinational consumer credit reporting company, remarked: "How long you've held credit accounts makes up 15 percent of your FICO® Score. This includes the age of your oldest credit account, the age of your newest credit account, and the average age of all your accounts. Generally, the longer your credit history, the higher your credit scores."

4. **Credit Mix (10 Percent):** Just as diversification in your investment account and your income streams is extremely beneficial, a diversified mix of credit plays a nice supporting role in your overall score. Credit card debt, car loans, student loans, mortgages, and other open debts combine to form a matrix rating, showing you are not up to your eyes in one specific area of debt.

5. **New Credit/Inquiries (10 Percent):** This category also plays a supporting role to your FICO score, because it is subject to a number of factors. New credit accounts, number of credit accounts, and hard inquires (a deep dive into your credit history and contributing factors) combine to create a 10-percent impact (MyFICO, 2021).

## THE 15/3 RULE

A simple and effective framework to help build payment routine and help improve credit, regarding credit, is the 15/3 payment rule. Now that you have established the financial know-how and discipline to only use your credit card for purchases that can be paid back in full and on time, you can begin bettering your credit.

I use this tool every month to help work toward better credit. The first step is to find your credit card payment due date; these may vary for different cards. Second step, count backward fifteen calendar days from that due date and every month pay off half of your outstanding balance. Third step, as the billing cycle goes on, pay the remaining balance three days before your statement is due.

This simple framework, often misunderstood to be utilized in order to register two payments per month, actually provides benefits by reducing your credit card utilization ratio. Remember, the utilization ratio accounts for 30 percent, and by using the 15/3 tool, your reported utilization ratio will be lower on the reporting date (Gallo 2021).

For an added benefit, this tool has helped me build routine into my monthly cadence of finances. Routines are the key to success, and when you can adhere to a routine of progressing your financial situation, your credit score will thank you.

## THE UPS AND DOWNS

As you may have learned in college, it is easy to tank your grade in a class with a few bad grades, but trying to resurrect your grade is a nearly impossible task. Credit mirrors this model pretty well; everything is good until it is not.

Credit card companies don't care if you have enough money to pay your rent or buy groceries; all they care about is being paid the amount owed to them every month. Ideally, they would actually prefer that you not have the cash to back your purchases so that you continue to purchase using their card and stacking up high interest payments. This chapter is positioned just so in this book because a credit card, or utilizing credit, can only come when all other elements of your personal finance strategy are in order.

A poor spending mindset can easily leverage a credit card for the worst, spending carelessly on the idea that you can always pay it back later. Wrong. Now that you have adjusted your outflow of money, it becomes clear the amount of money you actually have for spending and utilization. Credit cards can quickly become the downfall of people of all ages, and that is why you see an exorbitant amount of debt consolidation commercials. They wouldn't be so frequent if it weren't such a rampant problem.

Clawing back your credit score is a challenge, but not because it is an intricate task. It is only a challenge because first it requires the shifted value structure to back the proper actions, but also because it cannot be changed overnight. As much as we might want to speed up the days and months to increase your adult report card, it just does not happen that way.

## NOT ALL BAD

Now that we have deconstructed the scary topic of using credit, it is important to realize that credit is a positive tool for wealth building, but only when it is used responsibly to take advantage of benefits and purchasing on credit. Your credit is a reflection of your decisions; you have the power to change your decision and in turn change your credit. As much as some finance gurus and fearmongering commercials might lead you to believe, credit building is not difficult. Simply put, do not spend money you do not have currently, or will not have within this credit cycle. Pretty cut-and-dry.

Increasing credit scores will lead to improved credit lines on credit cards, higher lines of credit for a house, and smaller percentage rates on loans. The exclusivity of these benefits is not a tough bridge to cross; it requires the determination and routine to build your credit month over month. Higher credit lines with lower interest rates can open a whole new world for those looking to leverage credit for things such as real estate investing or any other credit-driven opportunity.

For every financial topic you learn about, three more unveil themselves to you. Credit is no different; the more questions you ask about credit, the more avenues to leveraging credit will surface, all for your betterment. It is your responsibility to put the work into the relationship of credit. You must show up on time for your movie dates, and you must be attentive to the ebbs and flows of the relationship. Don't make promises you cannot make good on.

This journey, just like a long-term relationship, does not happen overnight, but it damn well can come crashing down with a few bad decisions. Spend wisely and leverage up.

**CHAPTER 7:**

# Cows Out to Pasture

---

*"The problem is, [retirement] was created at a time when people started working at eighteen. Most people did not go to college; most people started their employment at eighteen and worked until they were in their early to midsixties and retired with a pension…and by seventy-two they were dead. That worked great financially for the government"*

-ERIC BROTMAN, ON *MILLENNIAL MONEY PODCAST*

The concept of retirement is radically different today than it was when it was first invented. Much like any other concept in society, it is subject to change due to technological advances and innovation. Retirement has evolved into a much more complex structure that requires detailed planning and active knowledge, now more so than ever.

Just as manufacturing companies will retire an old and outdated machine that is no longer being used or is not as efficient as newer models, retirement was originally designed to phase out older employees from the workforce. Eric Brotman, Certified Financial Planner, podcast host, and author of *Don't Retire...Graduate* explained that retirement in the 1860s, when the average life span of a human was around forty years old, was designed as "a way to put the cows out to pasture." An employee who reached their limit of usefulness was discarded from the workforce to make room for a more effective employee.

Fast-forward to the 1900s, Brotman explains, there was a shift in the idea and construction of retirement. People were starting to live longer, and they were remaining useful for longer in their given role. Although employees were useful for longer, at age forty, they were beyond their most productive working years. When an employee reached age sixty, they were a waste of space in the eyes of management. Harsh but true. Physical work grew harder and more demanding, and employers were reaping diminishing returns on aging employees. Companies capped their losses of productivity at the age of sixty, and so began the new time frame for retirement.

From the 1900s to present day, the change in retirement is almost unrecognizable. People are retiring at age sixty-five or seventy and the production factor of employees over a career has increased due to innovations in technology and automation. Human assets in the workforce can provide value longer, due to the decrease in physical strain. Retirement has evolved over the past two centuries from a swift kick out of the workforce to a now-booming twenty-five-trillion-dollar industry (Compton, Game 2021).

The most recent, but outdated, innovation of present-day retirement is Social Security. Social Security was "...signed into law by President Franklin D. Roosevelt in 1935...a federal safety net for elderly, unemployed, and disadvantaged Americans. The main stipulation of the original Social Security Act was to pay financial benefits to retirees over age sixty-five based on lifetime payroll tax contributions" (History, 2020). With the original condition of people entering the workforce around age eighteen and retiring at sixty-five, the math worked for the Social Security program, but the workforce landscape has changed, causing a shift in this asset allocation lifespan.

With people living longer and therefore collecting Social Security for more years combined with employees starting to work later in their life, there is a gap in funding for this outdated system. Social Security is losing its power to support the retiring generations to a viable level and may very well be a thing of the past by the time younger generations reach the age to receive this benefit. This shifting workforce landscape, and a myriad of other factors, has prompted many employees to challenge the outdated equation of retirement: work to afford to stop working.

## THE THREE-LEGGED STOOL

The reason the Social Security model worked exceedingly well at inception was because it was not the main source of retirement income for individuals. The three-legged stool, commonly termed, was the retirement plan that was the gold standard: Pension, Social Security, and Personal Savings. (Compton Game, 2021)

This triad retirement plan was as synonymous to the times as when cigarettes were allowed in hospitals. The almighty pension was the reason you saw lifers at companies, which you do not see often nowadays. The pension was the reliable source of income for retirees. Couple that with the help from Uncle Sam, and you were able to live a cushy retired life. Personal savings were almost laughable in this equation, but the forward-thinking types did so to pad their cushion in their golden years.

Today, pensions are a thing of history books and the outlook for the younger generations to receive Social Security is beginning to look like nothing more than a dream. So what is left in that three-legged stool? Personal Savings. Say hello to your future, its name is 401(k) (for employees). With all the power in your hands for your retirement, you stand alone, like Peter Parker in *Spider-Man* when his uncle muttered these words, "…with great power, comes great responsibility."

Your future is in your own hands, which at first glance is a damn scary idea, but all it takes is a shift in the value hierarchy to see the power. If you say the same phrase, "My retirement future is in my own hands," with a different and more confident tone, it empowers you to take control of your life, allowing you to control your "whenever, wherever, and however."

## YOU ARE ON YOUR OWN (YOYO)

The once sturdy stool of pensions and government aide for retirement is dead. Dynamically, the retirement space has shifted and the simple truth about your future is that no one is coming. Not a single person will be interested in your financial wealth or betterment; you are all alone to learn and fend for yourself.

Now, you might say, "My parents or spouse will be concerned for my financial situation," or "My company contributes to my 401(k) plan; they are looking out for me!" Take a step outside of yourself and the bubble you have built up; the people who are outside your circle of care lack the interest for your future. Whether or not you can pay your car payment without eating ramen noodles to make up the difference is of no concern to the bank or your old college roommate, and old professors will not call you and remind you to increase your 401(k) contribution with a promotion.

Again, the statements in this book are meant to educate, help pull back the curtain on the world of personal finance, and incite action on the all those *Shoulds* in your head. You are solely responsible for your financial freedom and independence. You are solely able to increase your financial knowledge and literacy. You are uniquely positioned to win at money by utilizing questions and starting now (Compton Game, 2021).

**You are on your own for retirement.**

### SEEING INTO THE FUTURE

My experience with my 401(k) was exactly as I have outlined throughout these chapters. Ultimately, I was not sure how much I could afford, so I took a guess. My first iteration was a high enough percentage to receive my company's match and a little extra. Soon, as I got in the groove of paying my bills and assessing my financial values, I bumped my percentage up even higher, a bit aggressively too. Once I did this, I learned more about what I truly valued in my life.

By investing more in my 401(k), I was valuing future financial security over having more "spending" money each month. I made sure that with every increase in my percentage, I would always have the funds for necessary expenses and the float was made up in my investable income. Finally, I decided for myself that I would leverage my 401(k) as much as possible and made my biweekly contribution the maximum allowable amount.

Now wait, before you go and scoff at me and utter something about that being unrealistic—finance is personal. My personal financial situation is uniquely different from every single person reading this book. That idea, coupled with my financial value structure, allowed me to select that percentage for my contribution. Each paycheck, these deductions come out of your paycheck and are building toward a future goal; the best part is, you never see that money.

Out of sight and out of mind. Retirement account and other deductions come out and you receive what remains, meaning you do not have to transfer this money manually. Again, utilize the power of technology to solidify your financial mindset. The percentage that you choose to allocate is personal to you and your values, but I challenge you to reassess and reallocate in order to reach higher and higher each year.

The 401(k) (or respective retirement account) is one of many tools in your financial tool belt and plays a vital role in your wealth journey, but before you make any decision, you must remember that the other tools in your tool belt must be leveraged as well. Hammer out your financial values, drill down on your specific allocations, and remain steadfast; it will pay off.

## RETIREMENT AS AN INFLECTION POINT

The overwhelming sentiment toward working a job is that people wake up, work, and aimlessly wait to retire. Rather morbid to say the least, which is why you see an increasing number of people seeking alternative forms of work and rejecting the norm of set office hours and a cubicle assignment.

The retirement equation, for so long, has been rather simple: work for forty years, save money in your respective retirement portfolio, and once you reach a point where you can live without the income of full-time employment, you kick back and relax. But as our younger generations are entering the workforce, the climate has shifted to value freedom of time and experience over material items and assets, this shift has brought life to the FIRE movement.

We will discuss in the next chapter the concept of Financially Independent, Retire Early, but this mindset reallocates its value structure toward time, experience, and minimizing the limiting factors to those items, such as working in a fixed position. Eric Brotman explained in his time on the *Millennial Money Podcast*, that retirement is taking on not only a different form and function but an entirely new definition. He explained it should not be the goal to simply retire for the mere fact that you cease to work and become idle, but that you get to a financial milestone in your life when you are financially established and work becomes a decision.

With that type of mindset, those forty years of service in an organization might seem pretty bleak. But what is interesting about the shifted mindset toward retirement is that there is power in decision. The decision to continue to work for the thrill of closing that deal, or whatever your role might be, empowers you to enjoy the experience of working and not having to fret over money. Retirement in the new era of the working world is dynamic, it is tempting, it is regal, and it is achievable in a much shorter time frame than you might think possible.

## PASSION

Graham Stephen, our real estate mogul turned YouTube personality, is infamous throughout the finance community for his extreme frugality and his twenty-cent homemade iced coffee. And for good reason: coffee shops are expensive. On one of his four channels, he does a series of reaction videos where he reacts to other YouTube videos made by CNBC called *Millennial Money.*

On one episode in particular, he was reacting to a video of a young entrepreneur named Destiny Adams who explained in her opening monologue that she lived by the credo "once you find the thing you are willing to do for free, you have found what you will do the rest of your life." It is important to make a connection to purpose and retirement. As younger generations become more vocal about their value structure, with time and experience ranking higher and higher on that list, the idea of spending forty years in a job is counterproductive. If that person hates the job they are in, those forty years will inch by day in and day out.

The pattern of being a lifer at an organization is fading for young professionals, who hold on average 5.7 jobs between the ages of eighteen and twenty-four and 4.5 jobs between twenty-five and thirty-four (Bureau of Labor Statistics). Job changes are in some cases a ladder for acceleration of careers, or they are short-lived relationships due to lack of passion.

The antiquated practice of having less than a handful of jobs before retirement highlights why the ultimate goal always was to retire. It might have been due to lack of mobility within industry or some other reason, but careers with companies lasted longer then, as opposed to today's standard. Technology has facilitated a more dynamic workplace to transition jobs quicker and match making for higher career satisfaction.

Utilizing technology to find and pursue a passion and monetize it is what a large number of people are doing in this new economy. The path allows people to work longer for the simple reason that they are passionate. From there, the desire to retire does not seem as pressing because you are not slowly wasting away at job you despise. Nick Bare, founder and CEO of Bare Performance Nutrition (BPN), has been a longtime influence on my professional and personal life. He is originally from western Pennsylvania but has relocated his life to Texas where the BPN headquarters are located. There he continues to pursue his passion of health and fitness. In his book titled *Twenty-five Hours A Day: Going One More to Get What You Want*, he addressed this very idea of relentlessly pursuing passion through seeking knowledge and experience:

*I searched high and low for my passion. When I discovered nutrition and fitness, and through that found my desire to join the military, everything fell into place. I had a clear vision of what I wanted to do with my life. I wasn't blind before, but I couldn't see nearly as well until I found my life's passion.*

*Many people, especially those near the beginning of their careers, can't tell you what they want to do. Their minds are closed in regard to what they can do now and in the future. They have a limited perspective about the things they could choose to do, so it's simpler to choose to do nothing. Sometimes people are limited by outsiders' expectations of the life they should want for themselves. They think the only way to success is to go from high school to college to a job in that field. I never thought that was the only way to success, or even a good way to do it...*

*I am firm believer in experience. Place yourself in positions in which you can learn and absorb knowledge from firsthand experiences. These things will mold your perspective on life, and where you want to take yours. No one ever accomplished anything by sitting still and twirling their fingers as they thought about their passion. There is no substitute for getting out and doing it first (Bare, 2019).*

We are not meant to live cookie-cutter lives; we are to be wild and seek our passion. Although the fear of sacrifice might cripple some, those who question what more life has to offer, just as Nick Bare did, will reap the benefits. So whether it is living your life according to your financial goals to reach financial freedom, or simply pursuing your passion early on, the choice is yours. The time for analysis is over, the time for action is now, and the only way to ensure you are not just another cow being sent out to pasture is through direct action according to your life's goals.

Retirement as a financial instrument has aged and not evolved, but the logic and perception of retirement has transcended its original function. People are now choosing when they stop working; they are not being sent out to pasture. Employees and entrepreneurs are innovating and monetizing passion to reach the retirement inflection point. With the shifting landscape, ideas like the three-legged stool have been dismantled, thus leaving young professionals and Questioners the greatest opportunity to financial success—choice.

We are on our own, and that is empowering.

# CHAPTER 8:

# Start Your FIRE

———

*"The desire of gold is not for gold. It is for the means of freedom and benefit."*

-RALPH WALDO EMERSON

Do you want to work forty hours a week from the time you graduate from college until you are sixty-five years old, in exchange for a slightly increasing paycheck that may or may not cover your increased cost of living and expensive purchases? No? Me either.

Every generation has a battle to fight. Whether it be political or social, there is always a platform or ideology that gains massive backing in hopes of changing the course of history regarding a certain topic. As the tide of college necessity, with little real-world preparation, has come and gone, the damage remains: creating employees who lack financial knowledge and whose only path seems to be the inevitable forty years until retirement.

Challenging retirement is that new battle to fight for the younger generations.

As mentioned before, the retirement model is antiquated and damaging to the psyche. As young professionals enter the working world, the sudden crash of anguish falls over them when they realize working forty-hour work weeks for the next forty-five plus years, might very well be their life until that "happy day." But as Eric Brotman explained, the retirement landscape is ever-changing, just as value structures are shifting for younger generations.

Retirement is evolving to simply become an inflection point where a person no longer needs to work to support themselves but may choose to work because of a passion. If you look at the concept of retirement, it is simple, with only three major factors:

1. The amount of money needed to retire, or the amount of income streams to support your lifestyle
2. The amount of money you are saving/investing to reach the retirement goal
3. Time needed to reach the retirement goal

Simple math will show that in order to shorten the time needed to retire, you will either need to increase the money coming in or decrease your goal. The option of working longer is contrary to this type of financial mindset and is nonnegotiable.

## FINANCIALLY INDEPENDENT RETIRE EARLY (FIRE)

The FIRE movement is a money mindset adopted by people who seek to take control of their financial future. They seek to have complete autonomy throughout their life and do not wish to work until they are old. These FIRE-minded people see and capitalize on the value of time relating to money in efforts to live the life they choose. The FIRE movement means something different to everyone, but as a whole there are a number of tenets to follow in order to achieve this lifestyle.

Reducing spending is chief among these tenets and where the most progress can be made. Spending money is necessary for things like food, water, and housing to sustain life. Outside of those three items, everything is discretionary spending when you truly examine the nature of the item.

For most people reading this, you might think "I *need* my car to get to work" or "I *need* my morning coffee." Brace yourselves; you are spending too much money! Most things you believe to be necessary are actually just nice to have, not necessary. The FIRE movement is often a description in someone's biography on social media, or it is a catchphrase they throw around at parties. For those who are truly committed to this movement, though, they understand it is a mindset. It is not just reorganizing your hierarchy of financial values, it is the equivalent of challenging everything you have come to understand about money and finances.

The counterargument to all the questions that went through your mind about the things you *need* can be answered with this almost ruthless FIRE mindset. If you explain you need a car to commute to work, the FIRE response would be to move closer to work and walk. If you say you need the highest-speed internet for your apartment, get a roommate to reduce the cost. If you plead that you just cannot live without that one sweet pleasure, fine. Enjoy your small indulgences, but cancel one of your streaming services or do not go out that weekend.

The mindset of the FIRE movement is to first reduce spending at all costs. If you have your single stream of income, you need to cling to every dollar earned as if you will never see it again, because in essence, that is exactly the truth of the matter (Smith, 2021).

The expense and income gap is an interesting phenomenon that plagues people who see success in their jobs. Oftentimes, people will become accustomed to living on forty thousand dollars per year with expenses of twenty thousand dollars but after a great year at their company, they get a raise to fifty thousand dollars. What will soon happen is their level of expense will quickly catch up to their income level without the proper planning. Once that happens, that person is no better off than they were a year ago making ten thousand dollars less. Over time, with increases in earned income and the addition of a side hustle, the prescription for the FIRE movement would be that expenses and income get further and further apart, not closer together.

The hardest thing to do when rewiring your financial brain is to sustain your levels of living through the long-term, to continue living below your means to provide for a better future. The person who continues to live on a forty-thousand-dollar salary even though they have gotten a raise, only does this because they solidified their habits and values before the raise. This diligence will continue to build toward better and better returns over a lifetime.

## FLIP THE SCRIPT ON SPENDING

There is an interesting mental shift that comes with the successes of the Competence Loop. Once you rewire your brain toward financial freedom and you reassess your spending levels, you will see other aspects of your life being impacted as well. You will soon gravitate toward financial mindset podcasts and your YouTube feed might have way more suggested videos related to finance.

You will notice that you are well on your way in the financial freedom journey. Your mindset that once questioned your own knowledge and capability has shifted from self-doubt to self-restraint, and you are seeing your good money habits pay off at the end of every month with higher account balances and lower credit card bills. You are compounding not only your interest but also your wins (Proteus).

You have found yourself in the Competence Loop. The more you win, the more you want to win, and grow.

As this Competence Loop consumes your financial brain, your capabilities and behaviors will be vastly different, and your view on money and spending will be unrecognizable to your past self. Once you understand the power of time relating to money, you will keep a close eye on every dollar going out. Because you know that if that dollar is spent on something useless, it is money lost. Money that could have been worth ten times that a decade from now.

**Disclaimer:** The level to which you take your financial journey is of your own accord. Some people, like Graham Stephan, have taken it to the extreme, and his results are the proof of his success.

In one of his YouTube videos, he was outraged while reacting to the absurd amount of money a person had spent. He shifted, turned toward the camera, and in a semi-joking but more serious tone, described that he wants his viewers to become so frugal with money that every time they spend money on something useless, they should be ashamed and overwhelmed with regret. He explained that you should feel this way for the fact that the money could have been invested and taken you one step closer to your financial goals (The Graham Stephan Show).

His exaggeration in the video is a bit overwhelming, but the message is clear. As you become more practiced in your financial routine, your mind will flip the metaphorical script on how you view purchases and other items or expenses you once would not have thought about twice. Now, I don't particularly agree with the idea of inciting shame and regret for non-value-added purchases, but this is an example of how personal finance is different for every person. Let your value structure guide your decision-making, and let it drive how you react to slips in judgement, or slight deviation, from your ultimate plan.

If the FIRE movement had a warning label, this mindset shift would probably make the list, but this is not a bad shift. The overwhelming benefits that will come from your successes and compounding wins will only further drive you to seek new income streams and continue your questioning journey, all in pursuit of getting back what is most precious of all: time.

## EXPERIENTIALISM OVER MATERIALISM
Another noticeable shift that will come as a result of pursuing FIRE is the gravitation toward experientialism over materialism. The FIRE movement was created for the very fact that young people valued their time and experiences over material items and would sacrifice the niceties in the present for future freedom. This mantra will only be emboldened by your execution and pursuit of FIRE.

For the simple reason that you are committing to spending less money, you will not purchase that new sweatshirt or a gadget only to use it twice a year. When you do spend money from your allotted amount of play money, you will soon value taking a mini trip for the sake of memories instead of a sweatshirt. Experiences are forever, material possessions come and go.

The social culture of today still pushes the undertone of "Keeping Up with the Joneses" except it is plastered all over social media as opposed to looking over the white picket fence to compare. Materialism is superficial. The FIRE movement, depending on your interpretation and execution, is not a financial lifestyle of fun, it is only a clear reflection of your value hierarchy in action. For some, the degree to which this shift takes places is varying, but viewing items we purchase as "Can this benefit my long-term goal or not?" will transform the way you spend money.

## YOU CALL THE SHOTS

The thesis of this financially independent movement is straightforward: reduce expenditures while increasing savings and investments in order to not work forever. The FIRE movement as described by *Forbes Advisor* has three common paths for those seeking this life:

1. Fat FIRE is defined as being able to retire without altering your current standard of living. This requires the most aggressive saving and investment strategies.
2. Lean FIRE is the opposite—it means being willing to live a minimalist lifestyle (say living in an RV) to cut expenses to the bare minimum in retirement. Lean FIRE individuals aim to survive on, say, twenty-five thousand dollars annually.
3. Barista FIRE lives in between the two extremes. In this scenario, an early retiree plans to maintain more than a minimalist lifestyle in retirement and does so through a combination of savings and part-time, or gig, work. Also helpful in this early retirement scenario is a spouse who still works and provides health benefits (Smith, 2021).

There are infinite combinations of a FIRE life, but these three categories provide more clarity to this generalization of being financially free. Along with these categories of FIRE, you will undoubtedly be able to find suggestions for savings rates and plans to adhere to, in order to achieve these end states. Remember, these are just basic guidelines and are not tailored specifically to your life and values.

I love the FIRE movement for a number of reasons. First, it provides a mission for people to achieve something incredible for their life, providing more time to potentially pursue their passions or spend more time with loved ones. There are so many experiences to be had, so many wonders to explore, and when we have the ability to do what we want, when we want, it opens the door to all those "You have to see it for yourself" moments. Although the outdated phrase "Money can't buy happiness" is thrown in the face of people working hard toward financial goals, money can facilitate a better life, and create time and emotional freedom to create more happiness in life. Finally, the FIRE movement is empowering. At the end of the day, people, of all ages, who follow this path are in charge of their own destiny because they are the Questioners. These Questioners accept the challenge and life of discipline to break the chain of a nine-to-five job.

For example, an amazing success story of the FIRE Movement is Jackie Cummings Koski, age forty-nine, who:

- Accomplished her goal of saving twenty-five times more than the amount of her yearly expenses in 2018. With enough savings tucked away, she had the freedom to quit her job as a sales manager at Corps America in Ohio but chose to keep working. Knowing that she can quit, whenever she wants, is liberating, according to Koski.
- Koski started working toward financial independence after getting divorced in 2003. During the process of

splitting assets, she realized her ex-husband had $120,000 in his retirement accounts, about six times as much as she had in her accounts. For Koski, it was an eye-opening moment.

- "I vowed from that day that I was going to pay close attention to my finances and do things to put me on a better financial trajectory," she recalled. "I didn't want to be the stereotype of a divorced, single mom, especially being African American, so I did everything I could to turn it around" (Smith, 2021).

A story like this is not few and few between. They are growing in numbers, and they showcase the ability for anyone of any age to achieve this goal. Jackie Koski was not a young professional when she started; she was a seasoned employee at her sales job, and she was able to reach a point financially where she chose to continue working, not because she had to.

Now imagine how well-off you might be if you begin your journey twenty years earlier than Jackie.

## YOU ARE ON YOUR OWN - PART TWO

The FIRE movement resonates so much with my personality. It is the perfect mix of aggressiveness, discipline, and a bit of selfishness. The standard model for retirement is bleak and morbid, built over decades in exchange for ten or fifteen "golden years." The FIRE model is more than just retiring early, it is about having complete authority and autonomy over your life. You make every decision, you carry out every action, and you retake control of your life.

Becoming the master of your own destiny might sound like a grandiose statement, but just as Jackie Koski and so many other people have done, it is within reach. By setting a course for your future, guided by your financial value hierarchy and supplemented by inquisitiveness, you will reach the end state you seek.

The magnitude of this idea cannot be overstated: you are on your own, and that's a good thing.

# CHAPTER 9:

# A Sturdy Table

---

In 2021, one in three Americans works a side hustle and 24 percent of Americans plan to start a side hustle this year. If you made an extra fifty dollars per day, outside of your full-time job, for 250 days out of the year, you would make an extra $12,500 per year. This is how small wins add up to huge success over the long-term. The addition of a secondary income stream, big or small, will be amaze you with its impact on your financial journey. The additional money incoming is one of the benefits to a side hustle as well as income diversification (Team Zapier).

Diversification is usually a term used in conversation about investing and addressing volatility. The idea of diversification presents a basic tenet that can be applied to a number of other items. When you diversify your financial portfolio, you are mitigating one specific risk, or volatility, by using other instruments to counterbalance those risks. So instead of being exposed to the risk of one stock in a portfolio, you might purchase a number of other stocks from different industries, and of varying sizes. Because if one stock you are holding goes bankrupt, your entire portfolio won't be bust. It will be able to absorb the blow because of the various other investments.

Just as you diversify your financial portfolio, you must also diversify your income streams, explained Robert Kiyosaki, world-renowned author and businessman. In his bestselling book, *Rich Dad Poor Dad*, Kiyosaki detailed differing perspectives regarding money using two juxtaposed people in his life. His "Rich Dad" was his friend's father, who was a self-starter, an entrepreneur who challenged the traditional money structure and questioned every aspect of life. This resulted in him being not just monetarily wealthy, but intellectually rich, the prime example of a Questioner. Kiyosaki's "Poor Dad" was his biological father, who lived by societal norms and accepted the unavailing waves of mediocrity. He was neither monetarily rich nor fiscally intelligent; he was not a Questioner (Kiyosaki).

## DIVERSIFICATION

Throughout his educational years, while shadowing his Rich Dad, Robert Kiyosaki learned, and then he imparted the knowledge of income streams to his reader. He explained that there are three types of income streams:

- Portfolio
- Passive
- Earned

**Portfolio** income is the appreciation of investment instruments or capital gains. As was explained in the previous chapter, portfolio income favors those who begin early and invest often.

**Passive** income comes in on a regular basis from returning investments, such as rental income from rental properties. Passive income requires upfront investment and potentially some upkeep, but the allure to this income stream is the passivity: sit back and collect.

**Earned** income for most young professionals will be the main or only source of income directly out of school. Unfortunately, even though a salaried positioned appears to be a relatively concrete source of income, everything is subject to change in the blink of an eye. Therefore, if your entire financial dependence is reliant upon your biweekly paycheck from your employer, your income would decrease 100 percent if you were to be let go. Thus, you are extremely exposed to job market volatility. To limit your exposure to the unknown volatility of the earned income stream, you can utilize your skills or passion to supplement your income (Kiyosaki).

Imagine your financial well-being as a table. If you solely relied on your earned income and something were to occur, that income stream would be disrupted, that leg would fail. Ultimately, your entire table would collapse. But, if your financial table was held up by three, five, or even seven legs and one of them snapped, your table might be a little wobbly but would remain intact and standing.

The creation of multiple income streams helps fortify your financial table, and the lowest barrier to entry is an easy side hustle.

Starting a side hustle has become popularized by online gurus and people trying to sell courses, but it does not need to be anything extraordinary. It is simply an additional source of income. Once the realization that you are on your own in life, doing anything or any job that you can in order to better your financial position will soon be the topic of many of your thoughts.

## CART BEFORE THE HORSE

Modern society has become, and will continue to be, a culture of addition: a8dd-ons for your vehicle, add-ons for your fast-food meal, add-ons for your flight home for the holidays, etc. Everything has become an addition to our already overwhelming list of responsibilities and expenses.

No one talks about reduction.

Reduction is truly an art. With the number of responsibilities, activities, social events, and expenses people incur day-to-day, it is tough to take a step back and breathe. This burden can be very taxing on personal health, physically and mentally. And soon you begin to figuratively drown in a life that is not really your own. The same is true for financial well-being; not only are we being stretched thin, with many additional expenses of living in the "modern world," but we are also being cultured to take on more money-making tasks in order to support our current lifestyles.

Adding additional income streams is a great achievement, but it has to be done for the right reasons and in the right environment. A side hustle, whatever form it takes, can only be done once an assessment of your current state has been completed. You can do this by asking yourself questions like:

- What will this additional money be used for?
- Is this expense so necessary that I need to add a side hustle in order to pay for it?
- Where am I spending money uselessly?
- Can the newfound money cover the necessary expense?

The one question that people never seem to ask or challenge themselves on is: "Why don't I reduce my spending and expenses?" Spending money can become habitual and can consume all one's monetary resources, fulfilling an endless list of wants and needs. Those very same people are the ones who decide to take on more work in order to fund these superfluous purchases. If that is in line with your financial value hierarchy, I am not here to judge, but that life is not sustainable.

While you are building out your financial strategy for the future, a side hustle can be leveraged for better or for worse. The additional money you are receiving in exchange for your free time can be used to fund investment and savings accounts. With each additional dollar, you will be inching closer to reaching financial freedom way earlier in life than others. Or, this additional money can also be used to fund temporary spending urges, leaving you subject to being a prisoner of pleasure. Granted, there will always need to be a balance of work and play, but how much you put toward one or the other is all based on your hierarchy of financial values and is ultimately your decision.

Adding a side hustle to simply fund additional expenses is counterintuitive to the entire theme of this book. Not only can you audit your personal expenditures and reduce your financial debts, but you can also add additional income with your side hustle. That is how you best widen the expense and income gap, making it a force multiplier for the future.

## A GATEWAY

Destiny Adams explained on her episode of *CNBC: Millennial Money* that once you find the thing you are willing to do for free, you will have found what you will do for the rest of your life. For some, creating a side hustle is often a project of passion, using a skill or talent they have developed purely out of love or interest for it. For some, creating a side hustle is getting a second job, for others it might be opening a small business, or perhaps livestreaming online to pull in extra cash. In any case, side hustles serve as a gateway.

For those who choose to monetize a certain skill or passion of theirs, this side hustle has limitless upside potential. If you become more engaged in your love of photography, you might start your own photography business, growing it year over year. Soon, your side hustle might match your nine-to-five income. This gateway allows you to either branch out and become your own boss as an entrepreneur or maintain your level of diversified income. Either way, your side hustle will only open doors, not shut them.

If your side hustle is taking a part-time bartending job or stocking shelves, this, too, is a gateway toward your future. But first, we must address the stigma of an hourly side hustle.

Once you begin working weekends and or afternoons after your regular job, you will have less time for other activities. You might not be able to go out to that concert or that after-work happy hour, and you may be judged by others for doing this.

Judgment might come in the form of, "She doesn't make enough at her job so she has to wait tables," or "He went to school for management and can't find a good enough job." You will encounter these judgments, either from others, or the self-doubt that surfaces in your brain. But, you need to remember the mission: to diversify your income while adding more money to the income stream. Even if those judgments might be true, you are bettering your financial position, and no one should ever fault you for that. You side hustle should be a reflection of your financial values.

So if you chose to find an hourly job as your side hustle, this, too, serves as a gateway. The gateway is adding additional funds to your savings and investment accounts, in order to love the life of your choice while others continue to be stuck.

## POSITIONED FOR SUCCESS

Newton's Third Law of Motion states: "For every action there is an equal and opposite reaction." When a side hustle is utilized in its correct form, to supplement income to widen the expense and income gap, it mirrors the laws of motion Isaac Newton bestowed upon society many years ago. As you add a side hustle, it will require more time, and you will have a decreased amount of free time—pretty simple.

Every day is limited to twenty-four hours; each day the sun rises and sets no matter your financial situation. It is now your mission as a young professional to venture out and take on a side hustle and make the most of every hour in the day.

## "If you are born poor, it's not your mistake. But if you die poor, it's your mistake."

-BILL GATES

When your full-time job ends, you have the choice to either turn off your brain and capability, or push yourself and diversify your knowledge and income by way of a side hustle. Things will change, you will not be able to always do the fun extracurriculars you might have been used to before. But the time you might have spent out on the town will be used to build your knowledge base and financial wealth, which will allow you more enjoyment in the future; it is an exchange of time.

Whatever side hustle you choose, it will position you toward success the very day you begin work. You will consciously be making the decision to reject the life of being a prisoner of pleasure, and you will soon reap the rewards of shifting values, capability, and environment.

# CHAPTER 10:

# The Thrifty Wealth Builder

———

If you came across a penny lying on the ground, would you pick it up?

So far, we have covered a number of topics cascading from adding a side hustle to supplement your investable income all the way down to talking about feelings and financial values. These topics are very mainstream to cover in the personal finance space, and for every article and book you can find about those topics, there are fifteen more about the same thing. Where a lot of these other books fall short is by failing to look for the small ways to save money, finding more pennies.

Aside from utilizing a Roth IRA and beginning your saving journey with the 30-30-40 benchmark, there are more crumbs to be picked up in the world of building wealth. These crumb-finding activities and habits, when coupled with the powerhouse finance habits we have already covered, can add up to be greatly impactful. If you answered no to the penny, then you are also likely to be bypassing many other penny-saving hacks in your life. By examining your spending on a micro level, you can uncover many more opportunities to save money.

The Questioning mindset, which you have come to develop or further solidify, will help with identifying these great money-saving techniques. You will soon begin to question every financial transaction you have and to search for ways to save money or reduce your overall expenditure in any way possible. Oftentimes you hear that "rich" people do not stay rich by paying unnecessary expenses; this is very true. The hard-earned money you receive from your nine-to-five and your passive income stream(s) is valuable, and you should do anything to retain as much as possible.

Picking up a penny on the ground is not sexy, and seemingly useless, but let's say every time you went into a store you found a penny. Would you pick all those pennies up? Those pennies start to add up, and quickly. To help supercharge your financial journey, seek out all those pennies.

### NEVER PAY FULL PRICE, INVEST THE DIFFERENCE

As consumers, we are accustomed to seeing a price and if we value that good or service enough we are willing to pay the asking price from that retailer or service provider. There are purchases that are needed to sustain day-to-day life. So stopping the spending of all money is not the solution for personal financial success. Even though we need to spend money on goods and services to survive and maintain our health, as well as spend money on leisure activities, you can still manage to spend the money on those things and do something beneficial for your portfolio.

Let's say you have been eyeing up a new jacket or pair of shoes for a while now. Old you would not have thought twice, you would have smashed the "Buy Now" button and maybe wallowed in your buyer remorse three days later when the package arrived. Let's say this item you are looking to purchase is $49.99 with tax and shipping. Mentally, you have prepared yourself and accepted the obligation to pay this certain price at that moment in time.

But wait! Utilize technology to your advantage again and go search for a coupon or other type of discount code. Oftentimes you can utilize websites to leverage savings on your purchase, which is great. You have taken five more minutes to do your due diligence and found a ten-dollar-off coupon on this item. After you input your code, your new total drops to $39.99; what a great feeling, you really got it over on the seller and you got your new pair of shoes. This is where most people stop and continue on their path to living in the middle.

Before you found the coupon code, you were ready and willing to pay the full price of $49.99. You need to take advantage of those ten dollars you got back. This money-saving tip is highly psychological; we want to feel good about our purchase and leave it at the perceived savings. You really do right by yourself, and strike the balance of life, when you take the ten dollars you were already prepared to spend and either save or invest it. Utilize your psyche in your favor; not only have you gotten your fix of shopping and saved ten dollars, but you have now invested ten dollars toward your future.

No amount is too small to invest and build toward to the future.

## CUSTOMER LOYALTY PROGRAMS

Consumer durable stores across all industries have Customer Loyalty programs, which are often waived off at the register when the employee asks if you would like to sign up for their program. These programs are another way to pick up those pennies. In this section we are going to focus specifically on grocery stores and gas stations that have a partnership. When you sign up for these programs, any money you spend on groceries, a percentage goes toward money off your gas bill and vice versa—not bad.

When you begin to realize the power of these savings and their compounding effect, what was once thought of as an inconvenience to cross that highway to get to a certain gas station will seem much more enticing. Prior to your penny-pinching endeavors, it might have been easier to pop into whatever gas station was closest when your light blinks on, but now the success is in the planning. Preparation and planning help to mitigate these scenarios, and when prioritizing savings, planning your day or weekend errands will include a dedicated stop on the route for these savings.

It almost becomes a no-brainer when you realize the power of these savings. You have to spend money on groceries and gas anyway, so why not take advantage of those "pennies on the ground," which will add up ever so quickly. What is amazing about these thrifty spending techniques is that the formula is almost interchangeable in different situations and all compound, working toward the greater goal.

If you did not heed my advice and enroll in a customer loyalty gas and food program, you are expressing your willingness to pay full price for gas and food. When you question how much more money you could be saving/investing, you should enroll in these programs; you get gas and receive five dollars off your purchase, then you can save/invest that newfound five dollars.

Remember, it doesn't take a fortune to make a fortune.

By the end this book, you will not only realize how much money you have been missing out on, but you will very quickly center your schedule and other routine activities about saving and investing, strange but true!

## BIG-TICKET ITEMS

At this point in your life while you read this book, you might be moving out of your parents' house or your current apartment to a different state; either way, you might be incurring some big-ticket-item purchases. These can range from a new mattress to kitchen appliances, and you will soon be forking over some serious money depending on how much you need to buy. We can mitigate some of those costs. First, we can check the internet for the best deal and find any specials or coupons. If you are able to plan far enough ahead, you can probably time it to the time of a seasonal sale, which even better.

Fast-forward, and now you have found the bed you want and found a coupon code. You also plan on investing the difference of the original price and the new adjusted coupon price. But wait, there's more! Most times those very same grocery stores, where you are an advantage member, sell gift cards. If you are putting two and two together and are following my logic, you are stacking savings on savings. Now, you will be buying a mattress online with a discount code and investing the difference of the original price, but now instead of paying with a credit card online, you use gift cards. These gift cards you purchase at your local grocery store will give you credit toward your next gas purchase. Since you are going to be buying a large sum of gift cards, you will be getting a sizable amount of credit on your gas. Now, stick with me here, imagine if you did this for all your big-ticket-item purchases like TVs, a bed, and furniture.

Savings driving savings.

What is amazing about this strategy is that there is no maximum or minimum. You can do this for the shoe purchase, for the bed purchase, and any purchase size in between. The level to which you execute this strategy is your prerogative.

Planning and prioritization are key in this strategy. If you neglect to get the gift cards on your advantage card, or look for a coupon code, you will end up paying full price with no kickbacks. By spending a small part of your day planning and using forward thinking, you can save on gas, save on your big-ticket items, and invest—all with one purchase.

## CASH BACK ARBITRAGE

Your new mindset toward your credit is drastically different than it might have been before. When you realize what an amazing wealth-building opportunity it can be, the world looks a lot different. A credit card can be, and should be only be, used when it can be paid off in full every month. Only then can you reap the benefits that are plastered on their ads. When you use a credit card as a wealth-building tool and not a temporary solution to a short-term cash fix, you open up a lot more opportunities to compound your wealth-building journey.

Remember the bed you really needed to buy? We are going to take this example one step further and build on everything we have learned so far in becoming a thrifty wealth builder. So, you did your shopping homework, and you found a coupon code; you saved the difference, but it didn't stop there. You invested the difference between full price and what you paid, but now that you have realigned your value hierarchy and are using your credit card as a tool and not as a limitless shopping spree, you also put that bed purchase on your credit card and will receive your percentage of cash back at the end of the billing cycle. With one purchase, you saved money, invested money, and even got paid to buy that bed.

Let's take this one step further; yes, we just keep going!

Same bed, same coupon code, same amount invested, and same credit card used with the cash back percentage coming at the end of your billing cycle. But with some very forward thinking and planning, you know you will need to buy a bed soon, so you prepare in advance. In this scenario, instead of buying the bed on your credit card, you go to the grocery store and get gift cards (when available) for the bed retailer and put the purchase on your credit card. Depending on what credit card you have, they usually have higher cash back rates for grocery stores, but the credit card company does not delineate whether or not you bought groceries or gift cards, the retailer is all that matters. See how all the small pennies are adding up, with just one transaction?

You are well on your way to picking up those pennies and making a real impact on your investment and saving account. Remember this step is predicated on your responsible use and repayment of your credit card bill, every month, on time and in full.

This multifaceted strategy has been a staple for me in my wealth-building journey. The money saved is great, and the cash back is twice as amazing, but what I have realized as I have matured regarding money is that this habit makes me disciplined with money. It focused my efforts to planning and being diligent with purchases. Even though I will always need to purchase food, gas, and things to live, I can do so while benefiting at the same time.

## BUT WAIT, THERE'S MORE

For the grand finale of this shopping example, there is still one more wealth-building strategy, which will prove be the most impactful. This final step is merely a result of all your other practiced savings tricks and proper planning.

Over the hypothetical past month, you have been disciplined and strategic in your shopping. For your groceries you have used your advantage card and credit card at the store, getting points toward gas and cash back. On your needed spending, you bought the bed using a coupon code, invested the difference, and put the whole purchase on gift cards that you bought on your credit card, and paid off in full at the end of the month. All your other purchases and expenses, you did the same and compounded gas savings and increased investments and cash back.

Once you receive your cash back statement, it shows your new reward balance of $250. You should be proud, but the final piece of the puzzle and missing link the chain of these financially minded tricks is not spending your cash back rewards.

Your cash back balance is essentially free money. It is a reward for money you have already spent and is out of your hands and is a fraction of your money spent. The savvy-minded Questioner will ask, "What do I do next?"

The most satisfying feeling in your wealth-building journey is when you use your cash back for good. Take your cash back balance and put it toward your credit card balance, so it will deduct $250 from your credit card balance at the time. At the same time, make a deposit into your high-yield savings account or your investment account in the same amount as your cash back. This is money you do not have to spend toward your credit card bill and is, in the loose sense of the word, "free money."

The first cycle you perform of this thriftiness will be enlightening; you may become addicted to this process. You will start seeing your gas bill decrease at the pump, you will start seeing your credit card cash back increase, you will start seeing your investment account compounding, and you will see your credit score increase as a result of your utilization and on-time payments.

Oh yeah, and you'll get that nice new mattress you have been needing and anything else you sensibly spend money on.

**TRACK EVERYTHING**

When I first started working full time and had bills and expenses to pay, I was pretty unsure how to manage it all. I was growing in my financial knowledge, and I was not sure how to best compile my accounts to paint a picture for myself every month. After trial and error, and a number of applications on my phone, I found a simple and easy way to do this: a spreadsheet. I sat down and listed all my accounts and holdings, all my expenses for the month, and my previous month's average costs for things such as gas and groceries. I was able to see all the draw downs on my money every month and I was able to see all the inflows of money, and exactly where it was all going.

From this point, I developed my budget for the month on another tab and made sure to sync this document to my phone for quick reference. A budget is often seen as a constraint to your life, a straitjacket on spending, and a restriction of fun to be had. Wrong. A budget is a nothing more than a tool to leverage knowledge and visibility. You can never improve a situation or fix a problem that you do not have knowledge about; that would only be wishful thinking. But with a budget, the budget information is knowledge from which you can edit your plan to move forward.

Rob Bertman, CFA, CFP, and the founder of the *Family Budget Expert,* explains the importance of tracking spending in the form of a question. "Can you reduce your spending by 10 percent?" You may have no idea where to start; there are so many transactions and categories of spending, that you might not have an idea where you could eliminate 10 percent. By utilizing some form of tracking tool that works best for you, it will empower you to take steps such as a 10-percent reduction (Compton Game, 2021).

Regarding a tracking tool, he equates it to a suit or dress. If you are at the store and you find something that catches your eye, you try it on and think it looks good but just needs some work. Next you go and get the suit or dress fitted to your body to make it a perfect fit and to fit your personal needs; a budget is the same thing. Just as we have said throughout the book, finance, and now budgeting formats, are personal to your life.

On my spreadsheet and budget document, I track all accounts from investment accounts to cash back rewards to cash on hand. I want to have complete control and command of my "employees" to make sure they are working for me as hard as possible every day of my life. Being detailed and meticulous about money is nothing to be ashamed of; it is a skill to be proud of, because those who lack the discipline to track their finances are the very people who accept the balance in their checking account at the end of the month as the way of life.

## MINDFUL SPENDING

The choice is yours; you either spend money without any other forces working in your favor or prepare and prioritize your financial wealth-building journey. These tips and tricks are not exceedingly difficult to execute and are easy to set up. The biggest barrier to this thinking is the "Prisoner of Pleasure" mindset.

Being a mindful spender is not a heavy load to bear, but it requires structure. When you base your purchases around your value structure, you minimize the room for any useless spending, ultimately keeping you on the Competence Loop.

Be mindful and question every transaction for ways to save your money.

# CHAPTER 11:

# I Wish I Would Have Known

---

Life is an amazing concept, and within this amazing gift of life, we experience, or plan to experience, a number of events that are said to be life changing. Some credit the birth of their first child or seeing the Wonders of the World; either way, words simply cannot describe the event with any justice, and you simply must experience whatever that thing is for yourself.

During my time completing my master's degree, I was lucky enough to travel to Peru and see the mystifying Machu Picchu. The pictures that I took and display in my shadowbox above my desk are an amazing reminder of the experience I had, but neither the pictures nor my poor descriptors can do any justice for the sheer shock and awe of the sight you gaze across on that mountaintop. Everywhere you look is another unique and extremely intricate detail that only complicates the schematic of the site. Needless to say, Machu Picchu is my "You need to experience it for yourself."

The most grandiose sites of the world and unforgettable life events can only be expressed in a lesser degree when being explained to someone else. The beauty of financial lessons is that you don't necessarily need to experience certain events in order to learn from them. When an elder or a colleague explains to you a story of their financial loss or budgeting mistake they might have made, the lesson is cut and dry. The exchange of knowledge does not lose its meaning simply because you did not experience it. This is the true power of capitalizing on questioning and others' mistakes.

As harsh as this may sound, you must expose other people's financial lessons learned and ensure that you do not repeat those mistakes for yourself. With time slipping away by the second, your financial aptitude needs a boost and the stories of "I wish I had known" are exactly what you have been looking for all along.

No one is lacking in lessons learned, no matter rich or poor. Every single person who handles money and finances has made a mistake along the way. Through the power of questioning and utilizing properly formed questions, this transfer of knowledge will provide you a playbook of the *dos and don'ts* of personal finance.

I was intrigued by this idea of how many tough lessons other people have learned, and how I could present them to all the Questioners reading this book. So I did just as I asked all of you to do: I asked.

Of the one hundred respondents who answered my survey, the group was composed of young professionals and seasoned employees across all industries and fields, some even in the financial services sector. I captured the most impactful lessons learned in hopes that these would be a starting point in your personal financial strategy moving forward.

## REAL WORDS AND LESSONS

1. *"Try to save as early as possible during the time you are truly independent. Once you are married, have kids, and have people depending on your income, it becomes harder. Save something. Even if it's twenty-five dollars a month."* -MS

Every dollar counts when it comes to building a nest egg. With the power of compound interest and time invested/saved, the outcome of this simple strategy is shocking to most. The excuse you will encounter the most when addressing saving or investing is that the person does not have "enough" to save or invest. It is not about having some ambiguous amount that is "enough," it is about starting with what you have and making it grow into something bigger. If you cannot build the habit of saving when you are broke, then you will never do it when you increase your income.

2. *"The principal of compound interest of a Roth IRA. Had I know[n] that at age sixteen, the way I would [have] spent/saved money would [have] been drastically different."* -RR

Contributing a Roth IRA is the best thing you can do for yourself every year. The maximum contribution per year (2021) for persons under fifty is six thousand dollars. Roth IRA is the better solution to a Traditional IRA, because a

Roth withdraws the taxes in present day as opposed to traditional, which takes taxes out upon withdrawal. So the logic follows that if you take the taxes out now, with your lower tax rate you will reap the rewards later in life when you withdraw.

3. *"Understanding long-term 'money goals,' as in, having a better understanding that the more I save the more I have later concept. Obviously, things come up when an individual has to spend money. Example, car breaks down and you need money for repairs. Going out on a date, vacation, buying something you've wanted for a long time, these are all things that can be accomplished easier without…if you can manage to put aside more money than spend on things simply bought because you wanted it. Considering finance needs are met with income."*

Long-term money goals stem from our financial values. Long-term money goals are critical to setting milestone goals and building off the small wins. Small wins compound and snowball into great success later in life. When you rectify your financial values, it will impact your behavior and capability, and ultimately your environment, now and in the future.

4. *"Every little bit counts—small savings at a young age build into massive savings into retirement and beyond… I never saw the money, so it forced me to save 15 percent of my income without ever realizing it was gone. (Buzz words/ terms in the stock/securities market; while I think I had some courses in college touch on this, I never truly understood until I gained interest and forced myself to learn… I think in today's age of credit and debit cards, a lot of people, including myself, struggle to understand where exactly our*

*money is going every month. That stuff was useful for me to cut out unnecessary expenses in the past."* -NP

This is a true Questioner! They knew there was more to be had in the financial knowledge space, and they sought the knowledge because it was never provided to them in life. As well they touched on "Out of sight out of mind," which is a powerful concept when it comes to saving for retirement and automatic savings. By utilizing technology to our advantage, we can break the habit of old and develop new capability and view of money and saving for retirement.

5. *"Start saving and don't touch it. The little things I bought didn't last long, and I wish I saved monthly and didn't take out as much money."*

Being a prisoner of pleasure will cripple your long-term goals. The impulse buy you had to have will not be around when you are old, but the ten extra dollars you put away will be, and it will have grown exponentially.

6. *"Understanding that a budget is not a constraint, but a path toward financial freedom. Also, understanding the value of the biggest asset: time."* -JCH

Monitoring money by way of budget is not a punishment; it is a powerful tool to unlock the unknown. This concept is not foreign. Many banks and applications, in some form or fashion, advertise budget tools to help find extra money in your accounts. It is not extra money, it just money that has gone untracked for too long. Stop the outflows of money and track every dollar.

7. *"Never have a car payment. Drive a POS till you can buy a car with cash. The more monthly payments you have the less monthly freedom you have."*

Living below your means now, to afford a nicer lifestyle later, has always been a theme for the financially forward thinkers. A monthly car payment is a huge killer to building your wealth. Dave Ramsey, financial coach and guru, suggests when buying a car you should follow these simple rules: it should never cost more than 50 percent of your annual salary/income, you should always pay cash, and you should never buy a new car, always used. Cars are a necessity for some, and when buying a vehicle you should adhere to these rules.

8. *"It may sound stupid, but stop buying coffees. You can make your own at home. Crazy to think of all the wasted money on coffee/food."*

There are a million variables and breakdowns you can follow to calculate the price and cost saving per cup of coffee. On average, a drink at Starbucks is around three dollars, compared to brewing coffee at home coming in at around fifty to seventy-five cents. Those three dollars mean a lot more than you think.

Not only are you saving about two dollars per coffee, which can be saved or invested, but you are saving on all the other implied or additional costs that might come with stopping in a coffee shop for a hot cup. You will potentially be saving money on gas used to get to the coffee shop, and you will be saving money on any additional purchase you "might as well" get while you are there, like a doughnut or sandwich.

A coffee is not just a coffee; take those two dollars and put them a high-yield savings account instead and a year from now tell me which one feels better: the compounded interest over a year of two-dollar deposits or the Frappuccino you got on that rainy Tuesday morning.

9. *"Financial planning is an evolving industry with constant changes relating to investment, saving, and insurance vehicles that a lot of parents are not used to or familiar with. For example, when it comes to retirement planning, a lot of young professionals' parents relied on pensions for their retirement. Nowadays, given that only around 15 percent of employees receive pensions, it is more important now than ever for the individual to take steps to plan for the retirement lifestyle they desire, and relying solely on their 401(k) is oftentimes not going to get them there. Due to their parents' lack of knowledge around evolving planning strategies and financial vehicles, and the fact that most young professionals rely on their parents' opinions prior to taking action, given they want the opinion of the people they trust the most, this oftentimes leads to a lack of action through the parents' suggestion."* -RB

We all receive different information from different people throughout our lives, especially in our developmental years. You should not discredit the information you are receiving, but you should seek answers for yourself. If your parents have been the sole source of your financial literacy, you should question everything you have been told for accuracy and validity. You are on your own for your financial future. You may receive advice and tips, but you owe it to yourself to get the best knowledge possible to provide a solid base for your saving and investing strategy.

Getting a second opinion on a strategy or financial move is not committing treason against your parents. You must do everything possible to create a well-rounded knowledge base from which to make a diligent decision for yourself.

10. *"I think a lot of people over time have fallen into what I call the 'timeline of excuses.' This was a quote of a good friend of mine... People always want to wait until after they get married, have kids, pay off debt, or whatever excuses they can think of prior to building their financial plans, while they are perfectly capable of starting now. It is my job as a financial professional to take the initiative to reach out, educate, and encourage young professionals to commit to planning before they themselves fall into the timeline of excuses."* -Robert B

Excuses are a coping mechanism for inaction. Excuses are just lies told to comfort a person for something they know they should have done or should be doing; excuses delay progress. The only way to combat the "timeline of excuses" is to take action. Action in any direction is acceptable at first, as it gets your thoughts moving a different way. You are no longer generating a reason why you can't, but now your brain is focused on how to make your action more impactful and long lasting.

Excuses will leave you broke.

Jeff Lerner, founder and CEO of Entre Institute, has built his brand and business on helping people grow their financial wealth through entrepreneurial routes. In one of his YouTube videos titled "Millionaire Advice for 20 Year Olds—What I Wish I Knew," he details the power and responsibility of a credit card:

11. *"Credit is not scary, credit is simply misunderstood. Shying away from things we do not understand is not a successful strategy to succeed in life, nor is it a smart strategy to go in blind to a situation you might not understand. The power of credit determines much more than a mortgage on a house but is overlooked for fear of missteps. A credit card when used properly and with discipline is another one of those power-ups on your journey."* -Jeff Lerner

Credit is built in your early years, the repetitive nature of never missing payments and using credit cards only when you can "buy it twice" and pay it off in full. Before you know it, your credit has been built, and it can be leveraged for wealth building. When utilized for good, credit elevates a financial journey to heightened success. When it is used for destructive habits, it tears down any progress made. Build the discipline, build your credit.

12. *"This is going to make you feel way better, but no one has any clue what they're doing, and most of us all are all just trying to figure it out as we go along."* -Graham Stephan

At the end of the day, we all start in the same place in life. We grow up, we learn some things, we find out that we need money to pay for things, and we go from there. Graham Stephan, a self-made millionaire who grew his real estate business beyond compare, explains in his take on the "I Wish I Knew At 20" video, that we are in the same situation in life. Some people are quick to learn about personal finance and they excel, and others know they should be doing more but don't know how. Both types of people are doing their best with the knowledge they have and making a go at it from there.

13. *"I wish I had asked more questions. I wish I had talked to more people about personal finance. I wish I had found the power of a question earlier."* -Michael J. Grus

The theme of this book is to ask questions to build a strong financial mindset, and it demonstrated a progression of the questions you should be addressing. You cannot seek answers to questions about investing if you have no money to invest. Your questioning journey should build progressively with success, and as you begin to rewire your financial brain, questions will become the medium from which you derive your knowledge. The answers you seek are just one question away.

The trials and tribulations we endure in life are an opportunity for lessons learned, and the true power of this life is when we share these lessons. The snippets above are only a fraction of the knowledge that is available from the people I engaged with and learned from along my own journey. The lessons above can serve as thought-provoking lessons learned.

These quotes touched on a range of topics we covered in detail throughout the book, but there is a degree of gravity that comes with hearing it from someone who has lived it and learned from it.

As Questioners, we are positioned to break the cycle of reaching an age where we can recite a long list of "I wish I had knowns," and now is the time to take the action to do so. There will always be lessons learned but the financial implications of learning those hard lessons can either be eliminated or decreased by learning from others.

The group of one hundred respondents to the survey answered a question that asked, "As a young professional, how would you rate your financial knowledge?" The results only solidified the three categories we introduced in the beginning of this book. The question was rated on a one to five scale, where one was "no knowledge, need help!" and five being "self-sufficient and thriving."

- Eleven respondents answered with "one"
- Twenty-three respondents answered with "two"
- Thirty-five respondents answered with "three"
- Twenty-two respondents answered with "four"
- Nine respondents answered with "five"

Eighty percent of those polled fell into the range of two, three, or four. Those are the Questioners!

The Questioners are here seeking knowledge and advice, they are engaging with financially minded content, and they are interested. In order to tip the scales in the favor of the

Questioner, we must act. Getting on the unicycle and trying will lead to change, and with change comes progress.

The past is the past and the future is unwritten. Let the words of others guide your financial journey and usher in a new era of financial mindfulness in your career and in your life.

# CHAPTER 12:

# The Questioning Mindset

—

*"Questions are powerful, they create connection, they drive destiny, and they inspire action. But the problem is, as humans our natural instinct is to say something, not ask something."*
-STEVE AGUIRRE

"Change is the only constant." The Greek philosopher, Heraclitus, could never have imagined how many Pinterest and inspirational quote templates his simple words would be plastered over by the twenty-first century, and the message of his words are simple, yet exceedingly deep. Although we seek to find central ideas and foundations to focus our lives and mindsets around, the only true constant throughout life is change. Change can be rapid, or it can be a slow burn. Change can be monumental, or it can be indecipherable. But change still remains change.

Change is what every Questioner seek—a change in mindset or a change in their financial situation. But change, big or small, can only be initiated when we open the door to opportunity by asking questions.

## QUESTIONS ARE LIMITLESS

Everywhere you look in the professional world, you see inklings of articles and snippets from posts that have a catchy headline about how proper questioning can develop your skills as a business leader. Utilizing questions is a framework taught to develop leaders within organizations to yield improved processes and results. Questions are being asked of employees and others of the like to improve a bottom line, but why is this same questing mindset not being taught to improve our personal bottom line?

In our personal life, we are taught to nod our head and take things at their face value. We are constantly asked questions throughout our life on every occasion. If we do something bad as child we are asked questions, we are asked questions on tests, we are asked questions in interviews, and we are asked questions at the doctor's office. The questions we are asked are one dimensional and serve one purpose: to extract an answer.

What is even worse is that throughout our whole lives, we are taught how to respond to questions, but we are never taught how to ask questions for deeper understanding and learning. If questions are being used to draw information out of us, shouldn't we learn how to do the same?

## BE CHILDLIKE

In a TEDx talk, Steve Aguirre, founder and CEO of Real Fun Growth, mentioned a study that was done that analyzed mother-daughter relationships. The research found that these children were asking around 390 questions per day to their mothers. Children are naturally inquisitive. They are so interested in life and everything that comes with it that they ask questions like there's no tomorrow. Even though the answers may not stick with them, they continue to dig deeper and ask more questions, almost to the point of annoyance (Aguirre, 2018).

Somewhere along the way, maybe in college or in the working world, young professionals and people in general have become scared of questions. We cower in the face of questions when we don't know an answer, and we shy away from asking others questions that may help, for fear of looking dumb or ignorant. But the only way to learn and grow is through questions. If you stifle your questioning muscle, your knowledge base will never grow.

If you really want to amaze yourself, track how many questions you ask in a day without putting extra emphasis on learning, then do the same thing the next day and push yourself to ask more questions. I guarantee you will learn extraordinary things by prioritizing questions in your day. So reconnect with your childlike mentality and question everything.

## INTERESTED V. INTERESTING

Your financial literacy journey can be expedited once you understand the concept of being interested versus being interesting. You have probably heard the old adage, "You have two ears and one mouth to listen twice as much as you talk." Well, this is that phrase, but formalized. The human condition is complex and overwhelming, and one aspect frequently sticks out to me, the urge to talk about oneself.

Let's say, for example, you are engaged in a conversation about a vacation with a friend. The instinct in the back of your throat is clawing at you, waiting to spit out how you experienced something similar during your trip. We seem to have to best one another with experiences, instead of truly listening each other. By being interested, you open a lot more doors in conversation than just the topic you are discussing.

Early on in my internship, my manager explained this concept to me by setting up a situation: You walk into a party, and you are making your way around the room. You know some people there from work or your social group, but as you begin to branch off and interact, you will run into people you have never met. When you leave that party, your goal is to absorb as much information and stories about other people as you can. After you leave, the group of people you talk to should say something like, "Wow, that Michael guy is pretty cool, but I don't really know much about him." Now let me clarify, you should not withhold conversation and be antisocial while prying others for personal information, but you should prompt others, utilizing questions to share their stories, insight, and lessons learned.

Even though money remains a taboo topic for some, this framework of being interested is still extremely helpful with these money-related conversations. You don't need to ask people about their current account balances, but by leading with humility and asking others about their financial lessons learned and any generically money-related questions, you will consume a wealth of knowledge. A question is a blank canvas, and when utilized by the interested Questioner, it is magnificent.

## BACK TO BASICS

Everyone has probably learned at a young age the information-gathering questions: Who? What? When? Where? Why? How? These simple one-word questions make the perfect platform to launch your questioning journey with anyone when gathering information to build your money mindset. These questions carry such great power because they are open-ended questions, they leave the door open for practically any answer.

Starting with these simple questions begins the foray into more direct, yet open-ended money questions. As you refine your questions to certain topics and ideas, you must keep the open-ended structure for your questions. Information becomes free flowing when someone is given a prompt to speak to, as opposed to giving a one-word response.

An example that I try to insert in as many conversations as I can when speaking with people about their financial journey is simple: "What do you know?" Not only is this question very broad, but it gives the person the power to decide what to talk about. From there, they might say five different things to incite five more questions from you. The goal is to extract as much useful information without leading the person down a path simply to provide an answer to a question.

A member of the gym, who would frequent the less-crowded hours of the gym, would often spend more time talking than anything else. Whenever we would see each other, he would be sure to stop by and simply drop this question, unsolicited with no direction. The first few times, I stumbled over my words and might have even said a random fact, but as time went on, I realized that I didn't have to have a specific answer, he was just looking to engage in conversation. So we did, and ever since then my first question to people I engage with is, "What do you know?"

The time and effort spent crafting your questioning mindset will directly impact the responses and information you find along the way. Dedicate time to work out your mindset just as much as any other aspect of your life.

### AH-HAS

Donna Brighton of the Brighton Leadership Group works with organization leadership to serve as a "catalyst for positive change and a liberator of potential, dedicated to enlarging leaders' vision of who they are and what they can achieve." Questioners are all throughout the world and this power to be a Questioner is recognized and monetized by many, but my favorite part about Donna is that her favorite question is "Why?"

Everyone can start with asking this question and build from there. The frameworks that she uses are not limited to business leaders, they are questions, and you can copy and paste the template in any situation. But first Brighton explains you need to do your homework by spending time shaping your questions, paying attention to assumptions, and utilizing open-ended questions to inspire action.

Understanding what you are asking is important, so by shaping your questions before you engage with someone will help direct the conversation. Acknowledge that wording of a question can carry implications. If you were to ask someone, "When did realize you weren't saving enough?" it implies that that person was not saving enough money to begin with, unless they had mentioned it earlier. Open-ended questions help inspire action on both parties; by asking open-ended questions, you might be driven to learn more and investigate further. The person you are talking to, while giving their response, might be making a list of their *Shoulds* in their head.

Questions offer much more than just an answer, they offer learning. Questions offer opportunity and experiences, and sometimes they are positioned just so that they trigger the "Ah-ha" on your journey (Brighton, 2021).

### MONEY QUESTIONS

You already have all the *Shoulds* in your head, and that is where you must start. As you begin questioning, you might find yourself on the internet or talking to coworkers about it, to ease your way into the rhythm. This is perfect, as any action here is a step in the right direction.

As you begin to refine your questioning strategy and begin seeking out new and different people to ask these questions to, your knowledge base will improve, giving you the firepower to ask better questions. One question can elicit a whole string of questions to come. Questions are the instrument by which we are enabled to seek more information; they enable us to elevate our knowledge and network, and they facilitate the power to overcome any and every obstacle in our path.

Humans are meant to be lifelong learners; we need to continue to grow our knowledge base and skills. We should strive for more every day and questions are the bridge by which we cross to understanding. Abraham Lincoln explains the importance of preparing for a task in order to achieve optimal results saying, "If I only had an hour to chop down a tree I would spend the first forty-five minutes sharpening my axe." It is imperative to sharpen your questioning mindset to provide success throughout your wealth-building journey.

# CHAPTER 13:

# Until Now

---

Negative self-talk is a grossly encompassing aspect of many people's financial mindset.

- I am bad at saving money.
- I have never been smart enough to invest in the stock market.
- I don't know how to budget, so I just haven't done it.
- I will never be able to afford to retire.

The path of negative self-talk is much easier to take when faced with opposition. It not only provides short-term comfort for your shortcomings, but it also provides justification for being average. Negative self-talk is the enemy of progress, and it can quickly deteriorate anyone's positive progress and forward-thinking mindset. By engaging in routine and degrading self-talk, your financial journey, and many other aspects of your life, will never change for the better.

Although you might be making some changes to your money mindset, the allure of negative self-talk will continue to lurk behind you, waiting for the perfect time to strike. No matter how successful or knowledgeable you become, negative self-talk will always be a constant to human nature, and the strategy to mitigate this pressure will be your key to sustained success.

The Questioning mindset opens so many doors for your financial journey and provides a wealth of knowledge and resources, but no matter the progress you make and the gains you realize, second guessing and self-doubt will remain, until now.

## TWO WORDS

The statements that opened this chapter are common thoughts of people embarking on their financial journey, and some might even be something you have uttered to yourself at one point in time; I know I have. As much as the human brain would like to regress to levels of comfort during the financial journey, there are two words that will help whenever times of negativity strike: until now.

The brain feeds off of perspective and direction. If your attitude and mindset reflect positivity and open-mindedness, you will find yourself in situations you never would have expected. It is easy to remain committed to your financial goals when times are easy and you do not have any unexpected expenses come in, but when your determination is tested, the statements above might creep back in. Your way to fight back is through positive affirmations of your direction (Smith, 2019).

The concepts of positive thinking and affirmations have been researched and studied all over the world for decades. Barbara Fredrickson, American Professor and Psychologist, refers to a concept that states, "optimism helps us build on our skill sets and utilize our inner resources…that the power of positive thinking could make you better at your job" and other aspects of life. She refers to this as the "Broaden and Build" theory (Clear, 2020).

T. Harv Eker, author of *The Good Millionaire,* outlines on the *Million Dollar Mindset* blog, that when you exhibit and live with a positive money mindset you:

- Look for opportunities instead of seeing roadblocks
- Recognize that every financial situation is fixable
- See the value of asking for help
- Accept that small steps add up to progress
- Turn your attention away from what's wrong and focus on opportunities for success
- Determine your actions and results when managing money (M. Ryan, 2020).

By adding two simple words on the end of any of your negative statements, it satisfies your need for self-loathing, but it ends with and provides resolution. When we add "Until now!" onto the end of the above statements and say them with conviction, they provide a better direction and outlook on the topics of each statement.

- I am bad at saving money, until now!
- I have never been smart enough to invest my money, until now!

- I don't know how to budget, so I just haven't done it, until now!
- I will never be able to afford to retire, until now!

## MORE THAN MONEY

Utilizing positive affirmations about money, and crafting a positive money mindset, expands the impact beyond just the balances in an account. When you direct your financial journey in the correct trajectory, positive outcome follows with it.

Money and the future of your financial wellness can weigh a heavy toll on your mental state, and when your mental state and capacity are consumed with worry it can impact all reaches of your life, including work and personal relationships. When financially stressed, your job can suffer the consequences of poor performance ultimately leading to stagnation in raises. From there, financial pressure and work pressure compound onto one another, an endless cycle of stress.

A 2019 Financial Employee Wellness Survey, conducted by PWC, published a slew of alarming statistics about money and its impact on employees.

- The number of employees stressed about their finances increased across all generations, particularly among Millennials: 71 percent of Millennials said that their stress levels, related to financial issues, had increased over the last twelve months.

- When asked what caused them the most stress in their lives, more employees said financial matters than any other life stressors combined.
  - Sixty-five percent of women and 52 percent of men said that financial matters cause them the most stress.
- Thirty-five percent of employees reported that issues with personal finances had been a distraction at work, and nearly half (49 percent) of those employees said that they spent three hours or more at work each week thinking about or dealing with issues related to their personal finances.
- Employees admitted that financial worries hade impacted their health, relationships, productivity, and time away from work.

Financial wellness is not isolated to outside the workplace; is it intertwined into every aspect of life, and it can become messy when not handled properly. By utilizing positive thinking and the phase "until now," financial stressors can be minimized by making routine and sustained progress toward financial stability and independence.


**THE TRAP OF COMPARISON**

The main source of most negative self-talk comes from within our circle of influence. In any group of friends or work colleagues, you will run into the Quick Learner. Remember them? They realized the power of money early on in their journey. Depending on their personality, they might even be very vocal about it, which can create shame for you and others. It is human nature to compare ourselves to one another, and when you are hearing the great successes of others, it forces you to be twice as critical of yourself.

Money has been, and continues to be, shameful for some, and it spirals individuals into the opposite of the Competence Loop. The Competence Loop comes when you mount the unicycle, when you venture out and disregard your fear and hesitations on trying or doing something new. The Shame Loop comes in the exact opposite fashion of the Competence Loop, and it starts with comparison.

Even though we have mentioned time and time again that your personal finance journey is just as it states—personal— we still find ourselves comparing our situation to others.

When we begin to compare ourselves to others, if that person happens to portray (key word) a better situation than ours, we recede into our shell and chastise ourselves for not being better. So begins the Shame Loop, where thoughts such as "I should have more money saved by now," or "I will never be able to invest like her" run rampant. Even if you have made great strides and rectified your spending habits and saved five thousand dollars, the second you hear someone has more money saved than you do, you begin your loop of shame.

Comparing financial situations is nearly impossible; every single person has different contributing factors, expenses, and inflows of money. To compare financial situations is like comparing DNA; it might be similar in the overall idea, but the minute details make each and every one different. Comparison to others is the kick start that sends you on the downward spiral of the Shame Loop.

## MY STORY OF SHAME

Just because I wrote this book does not exclude me from the trials and tribulations of comparison and shame. I, too, have fallen victim to the Shame Loop multiple times in my life. The most notable instance occurred during my time after my undergraduate degree and during my completion of my master's degree. I had recently graduated with my finance degree in the spring of 2018, and I rolled right into the start of my master's degree. Two weeks after I walked across the stage and got my expensive piece of paper, I was right back in a classroom doing it all over again.

At the time, I was living near campus, and since all my classes were at night, I decided I needed a job. So, I worked at Planet Fitness, purple shirt and all. I thought it was a great idea because I'd work part time to help pay my expenses, save some money, and get a free gym membership in the process. As much as I ended up despising my time working there, I realized a number of eye-opening lessons, both money and life related.

One time in particular, on a Tuesday afternoon about seven months after my undergraduate graduation, I was working the front desk at the gym. It was free pizza Tuesday at the gym, and I had just finished sorting out the pizza order. I had a few other tasks to wrap up before my shift ended, but before I went off to complete those odd jobs, someone I graduated with walked through the front door.

We engaged in some amicable conversation, not knowing each other that well, and exchanged the usual small talk questions. As we were speaking, I felt an overwhelming sense of shame creeping up the back of my throat, forming so tightly in the back of neck that I was almost unable to speak. I was demoralized because a person I barely knew from college had walked into the gym and seen me working a part-time job while he stood in the entrance describing how happy he was at his job downtown in the tall building. We shared our parting words, and he went on his way, while I stood there feeling numb.

He didn't know that I was pursuing my master's degree while I was working this job as a side gig; he was too busy going on and on about how happy he was and what it was like to make a nice salary. All he saw was someone he graduated with a number of months before, working at a gym. I couldn't hide my face fast enough, and even though I barely knew this person, I began comparing myself to him in every way possible.

- He was building his résumé.
- He was contributing to his 401(k).
- He was making so much more money than me.
- Maybe I would never be more than this front desk job.

I went further and further down this hole of comparison and shame.

To add insult to injured pride, I got a call from my manager later that day. I had since left the gym and was attending to all my other personal errands, when I heard my phone ring. I answered assuming they needed some coverage on an upcoming shift, but he asked me to come into the gym for a few minutes to discuss something important. I didn't really think anything of it, considering I worked part time, how serious could it be? I get fired? And from the interaction I'd had earlier that day, I might have even welcomed that outcome.

When I got the gym, I walked in, and my boss pulled me aside to speak privately. With growing concern, and almost a hope to hear the words "We have to let you go," he began offering me some high praise for my work ethic and highlights of my time working there so far. After that, he lit up with excitement and stated that from my review, they had decided to give me a fifty cent raise per hour.

I stared blankly back at him, for what seemed way too long, and all I could say was. "Wow, fifty cents!"

As he continued to explain (his whole speech was definitely rehearsed), I couldn't stop thinking about my exchange with prior classmate. I had just gotten a raise, and I couldn't even be happy about it. I couldn't take my mind off the comparison of myself to my classmates, all of them probably out there doing something other than working at Planet Fitness. From there, my time at the gym became rather cynical and resentful. I was regretting my decision to go back to school and work at a gym cleaning sweaty gym equipment. I was stuck in the Shame Loop, and I was doing nothing but comparing myself to others my age. I was struggling badly, both emotionally and with my money mindset.

Even after my internships and completion of my finance degree, I, too, was uttering the same phrases you might find yourself saying about your money mindset or situation. I had to take a step back and zoom out of the situation. I didn't reframe my perspective of working at the gym overnight, but soon enough I was challenging myself to save 35 percent of every biweekly paycheck.

I built myself a great base by doing this and reassessing my viewpoint on the job. I went from turning down shifts because I was miserable putting on that uniform, to picking up as much work as I could. I changed my perspective by changing my financial values.

I identified this part-time job as a steppingstone to my future. I would work as much as I could to bring in more money, but with that money I would refine and solidify my spending and saving habits. I wanted to cement these habits so that when I did get a full-time job in my career field, I would have the muscle memory to properly allocate money to my financial goals and budget.

My time at the gym taught me more about myself and what I wanted in life than I could have ever thought possible. I learned how to budget and save money when I was barely making over minimum wage, and it has paid off every year since then.

I never thought I was above the work I was doing, but I was trapped in the world of comparison. My journey was, and is, personal. The classmate I saw that day probably never thought about how I was working the front desk after he left, but I did. I terrorized myself and dug myself into a hole of self-doubt that I had to find a way to climb out of.

Comparison and shame might seem inevitable, but it is how you react to times of difficulty that makes your story a success.

## QUESTIONS COMBAT SHAME

Utilizing the Questioning Mindset is how to combat the Shame Loop and ward off the influence of negative comparison. The first words out of my classmate's mouth set me up to start comparing our situations. I really only knew what he was telling me and then assuming the best for him while portraying the worst for me, when in reality, he could have been battling crippling debt and working eighty-hour weeks. I had no idea because I did not ask.

Questions are the front-line defense against the shame that comes with comparison. If I had dug deeper with our conversation and asked him more questions about his job, I could have painted a better picture of what his actual situation was like and not a perceived situation. Questions do more than just provide insight into the lives and situations of others; they provide endless opportunities. The doors that can be opened when asking questions are unlimited, and all it takes is one question to potentially lead to the next step in your life.

Hindsight is twenty-twenty, and looking back on the interactions I had with people who were working full time while I was working at the gym, I could have asked more questions. I missed out on those precious exchanges of "I Wish I Had."

No matter your current situation, working full time or part time, being unemployed, completing a higher-education degree or going straight to work out of high school, utilize questions every day. If you are ashamed of your financial situation, ask questions. If you are tired of working your job, ask questions. If you have always struggled with creating and sticking to a budget, ask questions, and remember your positive affirmations to combat the negative self-talk.

Questions are the answer. They are the script to finding more: more information, more opportunities, more skills, more everything. Questions are your path forward.

# CHAPTER 14:

# The Playbook

———

*"You can't plow a field simply by turning it over in your mind."*
-GORDON B. HINCKLEY

I sincerely hope this book has brought clarity to the large gray cloud floating around in your head regarding personal finance and the keys to success for growing your personal wealth. Look around on bookstore shelves and online resources; there is an abundance of literature and information of the how-tos of personal finance, but there is rarely any discussion about the money mindset driving those principles and actions. As you have seen throughout the progression of this book, there is a sequence in which to address your personal *Shoulds*, as there are logical implications that are associated with each step.

Once you begin to see additional money in your checking account from not eating out as much or restricting yourself from tipsy Amazon purchases, you will begin to realize the potential of that newfound money. As you continue to grow on your money journey, your questioning mindset will be your guiding light or your True North. There will never be a time or place when asking questions is not acceptable. As you get older and you transition into bigger and more expensive life events such as buying a car or a house, there will be things you don't understand, and that is perfectly fine. Let your questioning mindset be your guide.

You might be wondering, "After embarking on this journey, seeking answers, and growing my financial literacy and wealth, when will I transition to being a Quick Learner?" I have to tell you: you won't reach the title of Quick Learner, but that is your secret weapon. As a Questioner, you will now and always have these tendencies and inklings that there is more to be had or done. You didn't start out as a Quick Learner (if you had, you probably wouldn't be here reading this book), and will not be one as a result, but you can be a Questioner. As a Questioner, your abilities and skills will advance and develop, putting you on the right track for your financial future.

This financial wellness journey you have embarked on will not be easy. It is always difficult to challenge ourselves, our habits, and our values, because we are, in essence, challenging our very identity. Examining and reevaluating your current lifestyle habits will be awkward and clunky, but when you push all those emotions aside and focus on your goals and values, these will ultimately lead to a shift in your environment, now and for the rest of your days.

To serve as a reminder, and quick reference guide, I have included "The Playbook." This playbook can be that quick reminder that the path you have chosen is justified and worth all the effort and time. As all good things come to a close, "The Playbook" will serve as our parting words as you embark on your money mission for the future. To my Questioners and all those who have come this far, accept this challenge and make the best life for yourself.

Because at the end of the day, you are on your own.

---

## THE PLAYBOOK

### THE MIND DRIVES THE MONEY:

The brain is such an awe-inspiring part of the human anatomy; the role it serves in directing our emotions and intellect is so incredibly complex and multifaceted. By acknowledging our mindset, we can produce extremely different results than ever previously thought possible. Everyone's personal finance journey is different, and we all begin at various stages. For some, negative self-talk will be the predominant tone and attitude at the beginning, citing lack of knowledge or insufficient capital as their barrier to become financially independent. Others will grasp the understanding of money but lack the knowledge and know-how to proceed for the better.

Take a minute to sit down and write out your emotions about money, either nervous, overwhelmed, or excited. Commit to paper your current feelings as well as your values. Identify what your personal value hierarchy looks like when you begin. As you foray into your questioning journey, you must constantly remind yourself of your goals and values that are driving this mission.

Soon your actions will drive your Competence Loop and you will not look back. Your mind is so powerful in ways unimaginable, but all it takes is one goal and one value to right the course of your journey. If you falter on your journey, remind yourself with that piece of paper; be direct and stay committed.

## STOP THE LEAKS

A boat with holes will sail no great voyages, and a portfolio with no capital will achieve no great returns. Spending money can be therapeutic, it can be a force of habit, or for most people they might not even know the true power a dollar unspent. With a well-crafted value structure and goal sheet in hand, your first step is to address the outflow of cash, stopping the leaks.

Any money that is not spent to sustain life and or is in line with your value structure, should be audited and reassessed for validity and necessity. Personal finance is personal, and throughout this book it has been made clear that everyone begins and ends in different places; what matters is that it fulfills your life and supports your financial wholesomeness. If spending money seems as effortless and mindless as breathing air to survive, there are ways to combat and overcome that need.

## STABILIZE, SAVE, INVEST

By addressing and minimizing the outflow of assets, you can now accumulate it on the other end. Hopefully that money is being put in a high-yield savings account making your money employees work for you as much as possible. Seeing your account balance build month over month is a sure-fire way to skyrocket your serotonin levels. When this happens, that will be your self-check that you are fully engaged in the Competence Loop.

Your small wins will soon compound metaphorically and monetarily, and you will be moving on and asking what is next. By first addressing your spending, it provides you the capital to save for emergencies and for your goals. The amount saved will be relative to your own situation, but saving money every month is nonnegotiable. Saving is the pivot point in your financial wellness journey; without it you are stuck. You must seek to stabilize your spending, save, and then you will be ready for the next step, investing.

### YOU CAN'T SAVE YOUR WAY TO WEALTH

Investing is the power up to your personal portfolio. With a number of external factors impacting your wealth, you need to be saving and investing to both solidify and grow your financial base. Your investment strategy is equally as personal and tailored as is your overall financial journey.

When getting started, do your own research; there are a number of low barrier to entry platforms that you can utilize to invest without the help an advisor. Leveraging the internet and technology will be your best play as you begin your journey here; take the time to research and invest not only your money but your time.

## WHERE CREDIT IS DUE

The next step in the judgment process of life comes in the form of credit. Your credit score is your adult grade point average, and it, too, can disqualify you from things such as credit card applications, loans qualification, and a whole list of other items. It cannot only disqualify you from certain amenities, but it can always hurt you as well in the form of increased rates or payments.

Your credit score is essentially a number to quantify to lenders and institutions how trustworthy you are to repay your debts. Just like trust in a relationship, it takes a long time to build it up and seconds to destroy it. The almighty credit score might seem fickle and indecipherable, but just as there needs to be time invested in studying and learning, the same is true for building good credit. A great credit score is the next item on the list of cascading boxes to check on your financial journey.

## YOYO

When asking someone about saving for retirement, you will solicit a number of responses. Some individuals are ahead of the curve, and some are of the mindset that there will always be time to save. But your questioning mindset knows there is something more to be done for retirement. Although picking investments, allocations, and percentages might seem like a foreign language after graduation, in some cases employers are picking up the slack from where colleges failed their students by providing seminars and financial education for employees.

You are truly on your own for retirement and your individual savings should be viewed as your only funding; any supplementary benefits are simply icing on the cake. With the time value of money discussed in Chapter 5, that should be all the wake-up call you need to take action for retirement.

The example we covered is so powerful that I feel inclined to share it again: per Acorns, with five dollars invested each day with a 6 percent (a conservative number) annual return until age sixty-five:

- If you start your retirement saving at age 45, you will have $71,210.47.
- If you start your retirement saving at age 35, you. will have $153,042.81.
- If you start your retirement saving at age 25, you will have $299,592.08.

Tomorrow is too late to start saving for retirement; start today because your future depends on it. When you reach the point in your journey where you realize you do not *need* to work, it then becomes a choice. From there, you will hopefully be pursuing your passion and thanking your younger self for the hard work and diligence in your developmental years.

**FINANCIALLY INDEPENDENT RETIRE EARLY (FIRE)**
The illustrious goal of retiring early is such a commonplace topic of discussion, but the actions required to achieve this goal are always trumped by short-term pleasures and unstructured spending. The goal to retire early, depending

on what you require to live off of in retirement, can vary, but it is still a tall order.

Being able to do what you want, when you want, and however you want is the ideal state—ultimate bliss. But to achieve this level of bliss, there needs to be sacrifice at some point. The decision to pursue this path is different for every person; some might downsize their apartment and only pack their lunch in order to save money, and others might sell their car for a bike and get a second job to supplement their income.

In all forms, the path to becoming financially independent is tough. To truly execute this task, structure and sacrifice are the theme, especially while others around you might not be following the same path. But remember that your goals for retirement are personal and aren't impacted by anyone else's actions but your own. The opinion of others is inconsequential to your lifestyle.

Fuel your FIRE with your personal why, as it will be the only guide through all the tough times, but you must sacrifice your short-term pleasure for your long-term happiness.

### HUSTLE

The creation of a side hustle can be done for the right or wrong reasons. After you have addressed your spending habits and are saving vigorously while investing for the future, the addition of a side hustle is simply to add to the funds incoming. Oftentimes people will take on a side hustle to only provide some extra spending money.

Side hustles can come in all shapes and sizes; they can be projects of passions that generate revenue, or they might be a part-time job at a local bar. There is no shame in a side gig because at the end of the day, if for no other reason, you can look at the additional money in your pocket and know that you are that much closer to your goals. For those who choose to develop and grow their passion into a business might even reap the ultimate reward: replacement of their full-time job. There is no time to delay; your hustle waits idly by, which can put you once step closer to your financial goals.

## THRIFTY HABITS ADD UP

Taking time to prioritize your spending and finding crafty ways to stretch your dollar will amount in a large way to your success in building your nest egg. These ways are only a few of many, which could be an entire book in and of itself. The main focus of Chapter 10, "The Thrifty Wealth Builder," was to be resourceful. In the world of finance, with so many powerful tools to be leveraged such as credit cards and loyalty rewards, one dollar spent does not have to always equal one dollar spent.

The utilization of buying on credit is a major factor here. This requires a credit card and proper budgeting habits, ensuring that you can and will pay off the balance each month. Every dollar spent, whether it is a necessary expense or a little something to treat yourself, should be audited to ensure that purchase is giving you some type of kickback, however small.

## PLAN, RE-PLAN AND SUSTAIN

Your personal financial journey is not set in stone, the budget you create in your twenties will not be the same as in your thirties, nor will your money mindset. Throughout your progression and growth, your goals will shift and adapt to your new values and growing portfolio. It is imperative to remain steadfast to your current plan, but do not shy away from a reorganization.

Time does play a role here. You should remember that although your attitudes and habits might change overnight, your money will not. Even if you declare you will save three hundred dollars a month, you still need to make that money and go through the process of saving that money. To that point, your strategy will need time to play out and yield results, so after two weeks when you only see minor increases to your accounts, do not throw in the towel and revert to your old ways.

Patience is key. As you begin to surpass your savings and investing goals, increase and adjust your budget accordingly as you grow older. Your journey to grow your financial literacy and portfolio is flexible and fluid, and most of all it is personal. Your goals are yours alone to achieve, so no matter the hiccups you might encounter along the way, remain invested and stay steadfast to your strategy; all you need to do it start.

## GO AND GROW

All good things must end, and as we come to a close, the only thing left for you to do is to take action. As the astute

Questioner, you now have the tools and framework to challenge everything you know about personal finance and the mental background supporting it. You can challenge and reevaluate your value structure, set long-term goals, and view spending in a completely different light. You will do amazing things.

Your financial journey is just that, a long and enduring journey. Unlike fad diets or social media challenges, this cannot and shall not end after thirty days and can't be captured with a simple post on social media. Your financial journey is to become as integral to your life and habits as breathing. The gravity of this situation cannot be overemphasized; it is make-or-break.

The life we live day-to-day can be overwhelming with deadlines and to-dos, parties to attend, and dishes to wash. Your money situation should not be the task you attend to after all else is done because in the end the same will happen to your financial future. If life and everything else comes before prioritizing your money future, you will fall victim to the cyclical nature of living in the middle.

No matter what age, we all wish to do what we want, when we want, and however we want, but that will come to fruition only if your mind is in the right place. So remember the most important lessons I have shared with you:

- Paying yourself first is the fundamental framework to beginning and maintaining your financial journey; you are important and so is your money.

- Time is not permanent nor is your current situation. The only path forward to combat the passing of time is to question and change for the better.
- After every small win you encounter on your journey, you will be ready to seek new information or goals. You have the power to change anything and everything in your life.
- Questions are the currency of power and with that power comes change.

Through the direct and pointed execution of asking questions, you can never lose.

No matter the ups and downs of life, you will always be one answer smarter and one step ahead if you follow these steps.

The only thing left for you to do is to ask yourself, "Are you done being young, educated, and broke?"

# "Choose Your Habits Carefully, They Decide Your Future"

-ANONYMOUS

# ACKNOWLEDGMENTS

———

Thank you to everyone who has supported me and become a part of this journey to author *Young, Educated and Broke*. What I have found to be true over the past year is that the author of a book is merely a gateway to share the stories of those who have impacted the author.

I'd like to start by thanking my family for being with me through this process. You were the ones who gave me the knowledge and platform to lead me to writing this book. It seems surreal that every decision you ever made as individuals and as my parents led me to this exact moment in my life, carrying on the transfer of knowledge. I want to thank my mom, dad, and brother for being the immovable objects in my life. To my dad, even though you used to believe I plagiarized my papers when you would proofread them in school, your literary guidance played an enormous role in this book. To my mom, thank you for making every one of my ideas and dreams just as important to you as it is to me. To my brother, Matt, although you might never understand why I do the things I do, thank you for always being in my corner.

I also want to thank a very close family friend of ours, Mr. Chester, who served as a role model and teacher throughout his later years in life. It is funny how we are never able to realize in the moment that a phrase will impact the rest of our life, but looking back, I realize how his words drove me to completing this book. He would always say to me and my brother, "No matter what anyone else does, they can never take away what you have up in your head. So learn as much as you can." Mr. Chester, I know you have guided my hand every step of the way, and from the bottom of my heart, thank you. I hope I made you proud.

Next, I would like thank Naomi who has helped me ride the ups and down of this book every day. From my first comment about it until the very last day, you have been my rock. Through the visceral highs and the impostor-syndrome-riddled lows, you heard my heart and made me reignite the spark I always had for this vision. Thank you all the way.

I would also like to thank my manager. When I first spoke to you about my internship, I never could have imagined the lasting impact our time together would play on my life. Every day that I walked out of your office I was a better thinker, questioner, professional, and man. Just as I will tell anyone who asks me about my time at Machu Picchu, I will say the same about my internship; you need to live it to believe it. Thank you for everything, SM.

Finally, I would like to thank everyone who contributed content to the book, everyone who had a hand in editing, as well as the amazing team at the Creator Institute and New Degree Press. At the beginning of 2020, I had an underdeveloped idea scribbled in a notebook and every person along the way played a critical role in elevating my thoughts into an amazing, finished product.

Thank you to everyone who believed in me and my vision and backed the campaign. Not only have I seen people from all stages of my life support this book, but I have seen a sincere care for my vision, and that is an irreplaceable feeling in life.

A Gerstel
Alex Domkowski
Alexander Hill
Amy Figueroa
Andrew Ziegle
Bailey Rogers
Benjamin Zimmerman
Brae DiPaolo
Brendon Masten
Burak Esen
Cameron Livingston
Casey Erin McCagh
Charlie Russo
Chase Tyler
Christopher Alico
Cindy Brigante
Colton Hearn
Connor Kok
Courtney Patterson
Dan Kubiak
David E Grus
Eden Bloom
Elijah Moo

Emily Egler
Emily Grus
Eric Koester
Flannery + Kyle Knapp
Frank Casile
Greg Gonzalez
Gunner Connor
Hannah Armor
Hannah Brasili
Hannah Pastorek
Jake Filyo
Jake Murtaugh
Jake Zambo
James Georgoff
Jarrett Noel
Jimmy Dolan
Joanne Grus**
John Ballantyne
Jonathon Mahalchick
Jordan Davis
Joseph C. Howard
Joseph Puvel
Julie Zorzi

Justin Ralph
Kami Davis
Karen Curtin
Keith Findle
Kelly Flaherty
Kevin Tregoning
Kolby Martin
Kyle Beveridge
Kylie Carlson
Lou Foss
Lou Tate
Luke Falvo
Luke Good
Mark R. Juzwa
Matt D'Amico
Matt Grus
McGalla
Michael Amedeo
Michael Fantin
Michael Sterling
Michael Urick
Michele Sheets
Molly Galbraith
Naomi Schwaiger
Nick Aiello
Nick Pensyl
Nick Walnoha
Nicole Cederdahl
Nicole LaFace
Nikki Mayers
Patrick Donovan
Payton Knupp

Rebecca Rosgony
Renee Brennan
Richard Grus
Ryan Filyo
Ryan Riesmeyer
Samantha Detore
Shamar Nelson
Shari Georgoff
Silvia Daley
Stephen Docherty
Stephen Spear
Steven Mezzacappa
Stone Haberstroh
Tim Schreiber
Timmy Mac
Trevor Hough
Tyler Condrasky
Tyler Sosnak
Victoria Kellerman
Vincent Centore
Zach Fox

# APPENDIX

---

## INTRODUCTION

Boomer, Jim on Henry Ford. "Whether You Think You Can, or Think You Can't…You're Right." *CPA Practice Advisor*, https://www.cpapracticeadvisor.com/firm-management/article/11575149/whether-you-think-you-can-or-think-you-cant-youre-right.

Fu, Chang. "32 Must Know Financial Literacy Statistics in 2021" PossibleFinance.com, February 15, 2021, https://www.possiblefinance.com/blog/financial-literacy-statistics/.

Hanson, Melanie. "Average Cost of College and Tuition" EducationData.org, August 15, 2021, http://educationdata.org/average-cost-of-college.

Wood, Sarah. "New Survey Finds College Students Lack Financial Literacy" DiverseEducation.com, July 15, 2019, https://www.diverseeducation.com/students/article/15105068/new-survey-finds-college-students-lack-financial-literacy.

## CHAPTER 1

Building L.I.F.E. Instruction Manual, Turner Construction Company (TCCO), New York, NY, 2017.

Cilluffo, Anthony. "5 Facts about Student Loans." *Pew Research Center*, Pew Research Center, 13 Jan. 2021, https://www.pewresearch.org/fact-tank/2019/08/13/facts-about-student-loans/.

Graham Stephan. "How I Became a Millionaire in Real Estate at 26." December 27, 2017. Video. 24:52. https://www.youtube.com/watch?v=sTpvUc9U6f8.

Hartmans, Avery. "Elon Musk Says College Is 'Basically for Fun' but 'Not for Learning,' and That a Degree Isn't 'Evidence of Exceptional Ability.'" *Business Insider*, Business Insider, 9 Mar. 2020, https://www.businessinsider.com/elon-musk-college-not-for-learning-not-required-at-tesla-2020-3.

Ionescu, Iulian. "How Our Beliefs and Values Shape Our Behavior." *Iulian Ionescu*, 8 Sept. 2021, https://iulianionescu.com/blog/how-our-beliefs-and-values-shape-our-behavior/.

Kess, Sidney, et al. "Financial Knowledge for Recent Graduates." *The CPA Journal*, 28 Aug. 2018, https://www.cpajournal.com/2018/09/04/financial-knowledge-for-recent-graduates/.

Lusardi, Annamaria. George Washington University School of Business. "It's Time for Colleges to Require Mandated Financial Literacy Courses." *CNBC*, CNBC, 28 June 2019, https://www.cnbc.com/2019/06/25/its-time-for-colleges-to-require-mandated-financial-literacy-courses.html.

"Undergraduate Enrollment." *Postsecondary Education*, National Center for Education Statistics, May 2021, https://nces.ed.gov/programs/coe/indicator/cha.


## CHAPTER 2

Belfort, Jordan. "18-25: You're Either Building Your Foundation or Destroying It. Very Little in between. Pic.twitter.com/mpfwwienoJ." *Twitter*, Twitter, 7 Apr. 2021, https://twitter.com/wolfofwallst/status/1379836786436833286?lang=en.

Feldman, Judy. "We Are More Comfortable Discussing Our Sex Lives Than Our Finances." *Yahoo! Finance*, Yahoo!, 9 May 2013, https://finance.yahoo.com/news/more-comfortable-discussing-sex-lives-102400204.html.

Grant, Kelli. "More People Would Rather Reveal Their Weight than How Much Money They've Saved." *Grow from Acorns + CNBC*, Grow from Acorns + CNBC, 15 July 2020, https://grow.acorns.com/more-americans-would-reveal-weight-than-savings/.

Marriage Kids and Money. "Tori Dunlap: How to Make Your First $100,000 (AUDIO ONLY)." June 24, 2019. Video, 40:39. https://www.youtube.com/watch?v=LzDwezveQ9s.

Schein, Edgar H and Peter Schein. "Humble Inquiry." *Humble Inquiry: The Gentle Art of Asking Instead of Telling*, Berett-Koehler, S.L., 2021.

Urosevic, Milan. "21+ American Savings Statistics to Know in 2021." *SpendMeNot*, 31 May 2021, https://spendmenot.com/blog/american-savings-statistics/.

Wolfson, Alisa. "People Are More Uncomfortable Talking about Money than Weight." *New York Post*, New York Post, 29 Jan. 2018, https://nypost.com/2018/01/29/people-are-more-uncomfortable-talking-about-money-than-weight/.

## CHATPER 3

Clear, James. "40 Years of Stanford Research Found That People with This One Quality Are More Likely to Succeed." *40 Years of Stanford Research Found That People with This One Quality Are More Likely to Succeed*, 4 Feb. 2020, https://jamesclear.com/delayed-gratification.

Compton Game, Shannah. "Build Your Path to Financial Freedom & Retirement at Any Age." March 2, 2021. *Millennial Money*. Produced by Art 19. Podcast, MPS audio, 38:14. https://art19.com/shows/millennial-money/episodes/fafe1ba9-7089-4fee-a4f6-44a6ad3d8126.

Gary Vee TV. "Why It's Hard for You to Save Money." December 3, 2019. Video, 4:33. https://www.youtube.com/watch?v=w_q8HFXG-ao.

KPMG. "The Number One Reason People Shop Online Is Because They Can Shop 24/7 - Transaction: An Ecommerce Agency." *Transaction*, 29 Apr. 2019, https://transaction.agency/ecommerce-statistics/the-number-one-reason-people-shop-online-is-because-they-can-shop-24-7/.

Quote of the Day. *Anewscafe.com*, 5 May 2009, https://anewscafe.com/2009/05/05/redding/6879/.

TheStradman. "That time I was homeless for 58 days." August 10, 2016. Video. 16:11. https://www.youtube.com/watch?v=187Y-J56hLNE.

Vaynerchuk, Gary. "Gary Vaynerchuk: How I Became an Entrepreneur." *Inc.com*, Inc., 16 Dec. 2013, https://www.inc.com/gary-vaynerchuk/how-i-became-an-entrepreneur.html.

## CHAPTER 4

Compton Game, Shannah. "The Secret to Finding Joy in Saving Money." March 30, 2021. *Millennial Money*. Produced by Art 19. Podcast, MPS audio, 41:54. https://art19.com/shows/millennial-money/episodes/de85f0c5-9275-4a00-b4e4-4a7985aa36b3.

"John F. Kennedy Podium." *Space Center Houston*, 24 Sept. 2019, https://spacecenter.org/exhibits-and-experiences/starship-gallery/kennedy-podium/.

Warren, Elizabeth, and Amelia Warren Tyagi. *All Your Worth: The Ultimate Lifetime Money Plan*. Free Press, 2006.

## CHAPTER 5

Acorns. "Imagine if you set aside $5/day until age 65." "*Instagram, 30 April, 2021.*

Chang, David S. "The 8th Wonder of the World - Compound Interest!" *The Art of Thinking SMART*, 21 May 2021, https://artofthinkingsmart.com/compound-interest/.

Eikenberry, Kevin, and Marcia Norman. "The Confidence/Competence Loop." *Kevin Eikenberry on Leadership & Learning*, 1 Aug. 2014, https://blog.kevineikenberry.com/leadership-supervisory-skills/the-confidencecompetence-loop/.

"Exponential Growth English Definition and Meaning." *Lexico Dictionaries | English*, Lexico Dictionaries, https://www.lexico.com/en/definition/exponential_growth.

Hewitt, Daniel. "Become a Smarter Investor – 8 Key Questions to Ask Before Investing Your Money." *Become a Smarter Investor – 8 Key Questions to Ask Before Investing Your Money: Financial Framework.* https://financialframework.com.au/resources/news-knowledge/blog/become-smarter-investor-8-key-questions-ask-investing-your-money.

Investing Authority. "Apple AirPod Max is $549. Someone with less tha[n] $1,000 in savings and credit card debt already preordered it" Instagram. May 25, 2021.

Lighthouse Investments. *Warren Buffett - Letter to Shareholders 1989 - Lighthouse Investment.* Sept. 2017, http://www.lighthouseinvestments.com.au/sep17.pdf.

"Retirement Topics - Catch-up Contributions." *Internal Revenue Service*, 10 Nov. 2020, https://www.irs.gov/retirement-plans/plan-participant-employee/retirement-topics-catch-up-contributions.

Schrager, Allison. "More Americans than Ever Own Stock." *Quartz*, Quartz, 5 Sept. 2019, https://qz.com/1700958/more-americans-own-stock-than-ever/.

Stevens, Pippa. "This Chart Shows Why Investors Should Never Try to Time the Stock Market." *CNBC*, CNBC, 24 Mar. 2021, https://www.cnbc.com/2021/03/24/this-chart-shows-why-investors-should-never-try-to-time-the-stock-market.html.

## CHAPTER 6

Gallo, Nick. "The 15/3 Credit Card Payment Hack: How, Why, and When It Works." *FinMasters*, 6 Oct. 2021, https://finmasters.com/15-3-credit-card-payment-hack/.

"How Are FICO Scores Calculated?" *MyFICO*, 4 June 2021, https://www.myfico.com/credit-education/whats-in-your-credit-score.

Resources.display. "What Is a Credit Utilization Rate?" *Experian*, Experian, 4 Oct. 2021, https://www.experian.com/blogs/ask-experian/credit-education/score-basics/credit-utilization-rate/.

## CHAPTER 7

Bare, Nick. *25 Hours a Day: Going One More to Get What You Want.* Lioncrest Publishing, 2019.

Caporal, Jack. "Average Retirement Savings in the U.S.: $65,000." *The Motley Fool*, The Motley Fool, 26 May 2021, https://www.fool.com/research/average-retirement-savings/.

Compton Game, Shannah. "Build Your Path to Financial Freedom & Retirement at Any Age." March 2, 2021. *Millennial Money*. Produced by Art 19. Podcast, MPS audio, 38:14. https://brotmanmedia.com/millennial-money/.

History.com . "Social Security Act." *History.com*, A&E Television Networks, 26 Jan. 2018, https://www.history.com/topics/great-depression/social-security-act.

The Graham Stephan Show. "Millionaire Reacts: Living on $158k In Grand Rapids, MI | Millennial Money." January 23, 2021. 18:23. https://www.youtube.com/watch?v=5GjKkRMGZrQ&t=72s.

## CHATPER 8

"Leadership Articles – Proteus Leadership." *Proteus Leadership*, https://proteusleadership.com/blog/?p=3216.

Smith, Kelly Anne. "The Forbes Guide to Fire." *Forbes*, Forbes Magazine, 18 May 2021, https://www.forbes.com/advisor/retirement/the-forbes-guide-to-fire/.

The Graham Stephan Show. "Millionaire Reacts: What I Spend in a Day in Beverly Hills | Nicolette Gray." October 20, 2020. 17:50. https://www.youtube.com/watch?v=aRlPOKhXaC4.

## CHAPTER 9

Kiyosaki, Robert T. *Rich Dad, Poor Dad: What the Rich Teach Their Kids About Money That the Poor and Middle Class Do Not!* FBV, 2020.

Team, Zapier Editorial. "Side Hustle Report: 1 in 3 Americans Have a Side Hustle: Zapier." *Side Hustle Report: 1 in 3 Americans Have a Side Hustle | Zapier*, Zapier, 14 Jan. 2021, https://zapier.com/blog/side-hustle-report/.

## CHAPTER 10

Compton Game, Shannah. "Build Your Path to Financial Freedom
& Retirement At Any Age." March 2, 2021. *Millennial Money.*
Produced by Art 19. Podcast, MPS audio, 38:14. https://art19.
com/shows/millennial-money/episodes/fafe1ba9-7089-4fee-
a4f6-44a6ad3d8126.


## CHATPER 11

Graham Stephan. "6 Millionaire Habits I Wish I Knew at 20."
August 24, 2020. 15:45. https://www.youtube.com/watch?v=B-
zwk7f9Ic44.

Jeff Lerner. "Millionaire Advice for 20 Year Olds—What I Wish
I Knew." May 1, 2020. 22:57. https://www.youtube.com/
watch?v=eoZ1LzefTws.


## CHAPTER 12

Aguirre, Steve. "The Power of Questions: Steve Aguirre: Tedxber-
gencommunitycollege." *En*, 19 Mar. 2018, https://www.meon1.
com/eng/tedx/the-power-of-questions-steve-aguirre-tedxber-
gencommunitycollege/.

Brighton, Donna. "4 Fascinating Facts About Questions." *Brighton Leadership Group*, 14 Apr. 2021, https://brightonleadership.
com/4-fascinating-facts-about-questions/.

# CHAPTER 13

Clear, James. "How Positive Thinking Builds Your Skills, Boosts Your Health, and Improves Your Work." *James Clear*, 4 Feb. 2020, https://jamesclear.com/positive-thinking.

M, Ryan. "10 Ways to Change Your Money Mindset Positively: Harv Eker International." *T. Harv Eker Blog*, 19 Oct. 2020, https://www.harveker.com/blog/positive-money-mindset-change/.

PWC. "Financial Statistics." *Money Habitudes*, 17 Aug. 2021, https://www.moneyhabitudes.com/financial-statistics/.

Smith, Emma-Marie. "10 Amazing Positivity Facts to Improve Your Outlook." *HealthyPlace*, 19 June 2019, https://www.healthyplace.com/self-help/positivity/10-amazing-positivity-facts-to-improve-your-outlook.

Made in United States
Orlando, FL
03 February 2022

14343973R00108